AF588492

BECOME AN EMS SPECIALIST

Emergency Treatment, Wound Care & More

Margo Gates

Abdo & Daughters
MIDDLE GRADE NONFICTION
An imprint of Abdo Publishing
abdobooks.com

ABDOBOOKS.COM

Published by Abdo Publishing, a division of ABDO, PO Box 398166, Minneapolis, Minnesota 55439.

Printed in the United States of America, North Mankato, Minnesota
102024
012025

Design: Denise Hamernik, Mighty Media, Inc.
Production: Mighty Media, Inc.
Editor: Katherine Chu

Cover Photographs: Shutterstock Images

Interior Photographs: Adobe Stock, pp. 12 (bottom), 48–49 (background); 911 Dispatch 2/Flickr, p. 11 (top left); Alabama Department of Archives and History, p. 7; Mark Wolfe/Wikimedia Commons, p. 20 (top); Massachusetts Emergency Management Agency/Wikimedia Commons, p. 21 (top); Maurice Falk Medical Fund, MSS 207, Detre Library & Archives, Senator John Heinz History Center, p. 55; Mighty Media, Inc. (project photos), pp. 50, 51; NBC Television/Wikimedia Commons, p. 8; ORLIN WAGNER/AP Images, p. 19; Petty Officer 2nd Class Johans C/Wikimedia Commons, p. 21 (bottom); Riverside County Sheriff's Department/Wikimedia Commons, p. 10 (bottom); Shutterstock Images, pp. 3, 4, 5 (all), 9, 10 (top left, top middle, top right), 11 (top right, bottom), 12 (top left, top right, middle), 13 (all), 14, 15 (all), 16 (all), 17, 20 (bottom), 22 (all), 23 (all), 24 (all), 25, 26 (all), 27 (all), 28, 29 (all), 30 (all), 31, 32, 33 (all), 34 (all), 35 (all), 36, 37, 38 (all), 39 (all), 40, 41 (all), 42 (all), 43 (all), 44 (all), 44–45 (background), 46 (all), 46–47 (background), 48 (left, right), 50–51 (background), 52, 53, 54, 56, 57, 58, 59, 60, 61 (all); United States Marine Corps/Wikimedia Commons, p. 18; Wikimedia Commons, p. 6 (all)

Design Elements: Adobe Stock (Polaroid frame, sticky notes, tacks); Shutterstock Images (bandages texture, dressing texture, medical supplies texture)

Library of Congress Control Number: 2024938326

PUBLISHER'S CATALOGING-IN-PUBLICATION DATA

Names: Gates, Margo, author.
Title: Become an EMS specialist: emergency treatment, wound care & more / by Margo Gates
Other Title: emergency treatment, wound care & more
Description: Minneapolis, Minnesota : ABDO Publishing, 2025 | Series: Talent to trade | Includes online resources and index.
Identifiers: ISBN 9781098295011 (lib. bdg.) | ISBN 9798384915065 (ebook)
Subjects: LCSH: Emergency paramedics--Juvenile literature. | Transport of sick and wounded--Juvenile literature. | First aid in illness and injury--Juvenile literature. | Medical personnel--Juvenile literature. | Clinical assistants--Juvenile literature. | Jobs--Juvenile literature. | Trades--Juvenile literature.
Classification: DDC 614.88--dc23

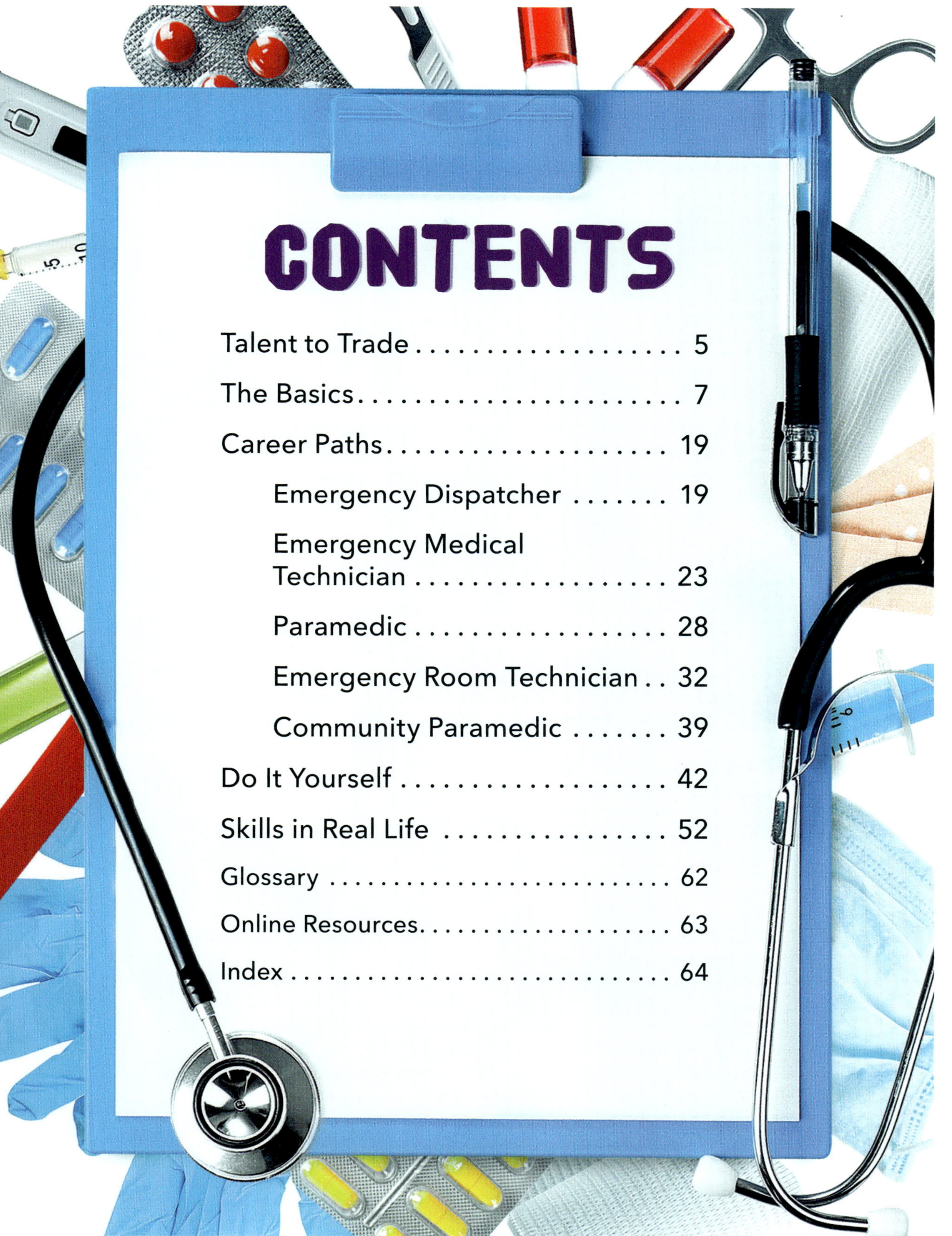

CONTENTS

POLI

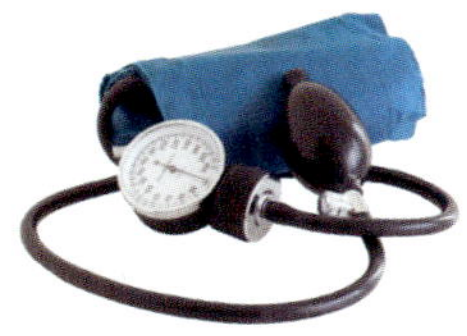

TALENT TO TRADE

Are you fascinated by the hurried bustle of an emergency room (ER)? Would you love to have the skills and courage of a first responder? Can you see yourself helping sick and injured patients every day? If your answer to any of these questions is yes, you might be suited to a career in emergency medical services, or EMS.

Becoming an EMS specialist takes a lot of training and hard work. It takes a dedication to the safety and well-being of others. But if you have a passion for emergency medical response and care, you may find that the dedication comes naturally and the hard work is worthwhile.

In this book, you'll learn about the history of EMS and the various jobs available within the industry. You'll become familiar with some basic tools, skills, and techniques used by EMS specialists. You'll find inspiration to begin working toward your own career in EMS. Finally, you'll learn a bit about the various paths to turning your talents into a trade.

French army surgeon Dominique-Jean Larrey invented one of the first ambulances in 1810. He called it the "Flying Ambulance." The horse-drawn ambulance included windows and padding for the patient.

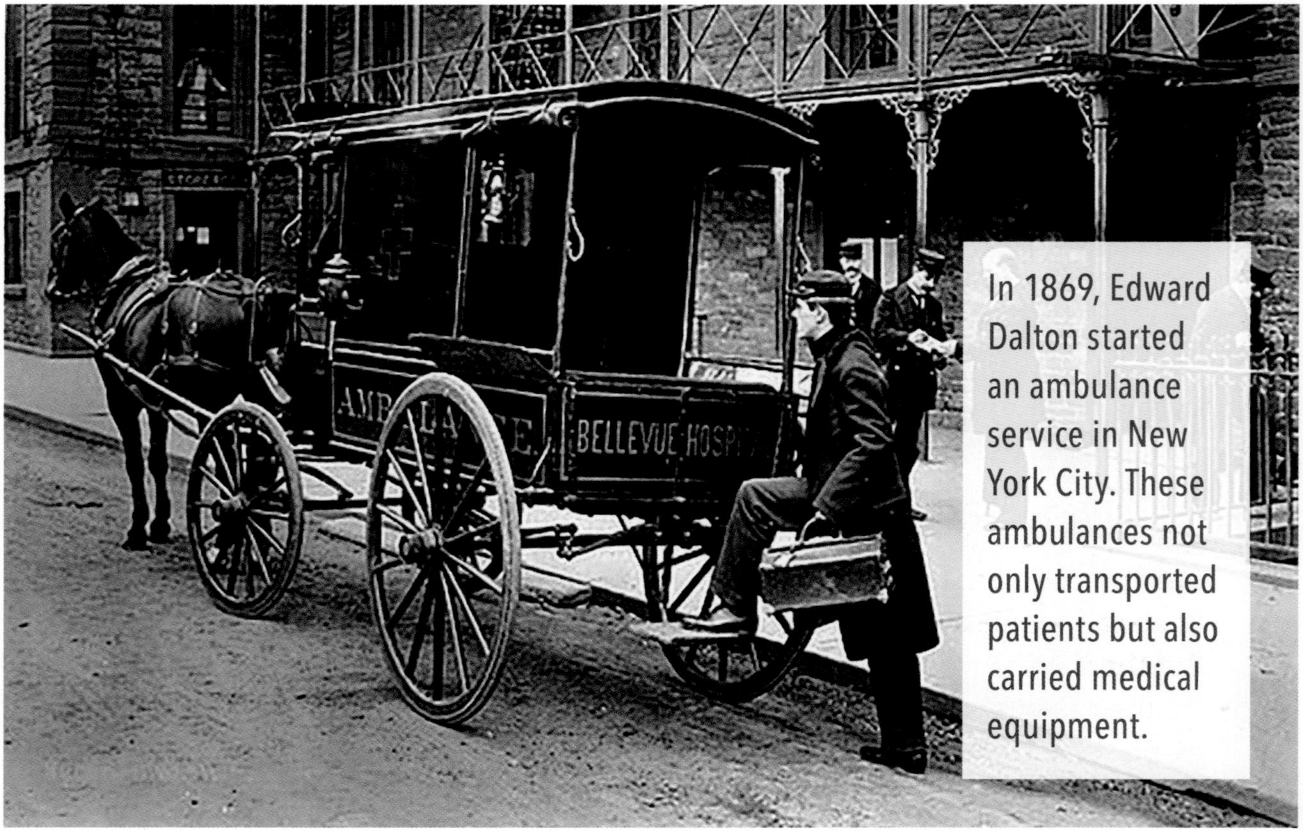

In 1869, Edward Dalton started an ambulance service in New York City. These ambulances not only transported patients but also carried medical equipment.

HISTORY OF EMS

In the United States, emergency medical services date back to the Civil War. The standard practice at the time was to wait until after a battle to help injured soldiers. But in 1862, Dr. Jonathan Letterman established the US Ambulance Corps. Its purpose was to treat injured soldiers on active battlefields instead of waiting until after the battle. This new approach prevented the suffering and deaths of many soldiers.

In 1865, the nation's first civilian ambulance service was established in Cincinnati, Ohio. A similar service began in New York City a few years later. After World War I, civilians formed volunteer rescue squads in various other locations. These included Virginia and New Jersey.

Over the following decades, emergency services were provided by a wide range of public and private entities. These included fire departments, towing companies, and funeral homes. Their goal was to transport patients to the hospital as quickly as possible. But there were no standards for the care patients received along the way. In fact, the general lack of emergency medical training sometimes resulted in additional injury to the patients.

In 1966, the National Academy of Sciences published a report. It was titled "Accidental Death and Disability: The Neglected Disease of Modern Society." The report highlighted issues such as the high rates of traffic accidents, inadequate training of emergency workers, and poorly equipped ambulances. Over the following years, the nation's leaders worked to correct these issues.

Senator Rankin Fite made the first 911 call on February 16, 1968, in Haleyville, Alabama.

In November 1967, the federal government started working with telecommunications company AT&T to establish a new way to contact EMS. Before then, people had two options. They could either call their local emergency services directly or dial 0 to have an operator connect them. In 1968, AT&T publicly announced that it had established a three-digit nationwide phone number to call for an ambulance. And in February of that year, the first 911 call was placed in Alabama. Dialing 911 routed the call to an emergency dispatcher, who relayed information to first responders.

Up until the early 1970s, the US Department of Transportation was responsible for EMS. But in 1973, Congress made the Department of Health, Education, and Welfare the lead agency in charge of EMS. This shift acknowledged EMS as, first and foremost, a medical service. That same year, Congress passed a law to provide funding for the creation of more than 300 EMS systems across the nation.

As EMS standards improved for prehospital care, hospital emergency departments were also improving. These departments received patients in need of immediate care. Early

The 1972 television show *Emergency!* inspired many Americans to pursue jobs in EMS. The show was about a team of paramedics who responded to emergencies.

In 1970, the University of Cincinnati established the first specialized program focused on training physicians for emergency medicine.

emergency departments were staffed by medical workers with no specialized training in emergency medicine. But in the 1960s and 1970s, leaders in emergency medicine began to set up their own practices and training programs. Emergency medicine become a specialty. And emergency professionals started training for the trauma of the ER.

By the turn of the century, EMS systems were strained. At the time, many people did not have access to basic health care facilities or clinics. So patients were calling ambulances with nonemergency problems, such as sprains or flu symptoms. As a result, ERs were filling to capacity.

In the early 2000s, EMS systems began to address this issue. They started implementing a health care model known as community paramedicine. In this model, paramedics provide nonemergency, preventative care to patients. The goal was to increase access to health care while decreasing the use of EMS services for nonemergency conditions. This would give ambulances and ERs the ability to help more patients in need of emergency care. Over the last two decades, hundreds of EMS agencies across the country have integrated community paramedics or similar roles.

Emergency medical services have come a long way from the battlefields of the Civil War. In the following pages, you'll learn what it takes to work as a professional in this field. You may even be inspired to start your journey to becoming an EMS specialist right now!

TOOLS OF THE TRADE

Get familiar with some of the tools EMS specialists use to respond to emergencies and help those in need.

EMERGENCY DISPATCHERS

TELEPHONE & RADIO

When someone calls 911, an emergency dispatcher answers the call. They speak to the caller by telephone to gather information about the emergency. Then they use a telephone or radio to contact personnel who can respond to the emergency. Dispatchers wear headsets that allow them to constantly switch between telephone and radio communications during an emergency call.

CAD SYSTEMS

Dispatchers use systems called computer-aided dispatch, or CAD. These systems help manage their emergency calls. When a call comes in, CAD can help determine the caller's location. It can also connect the dispatcher to the appropriate emergency responders. Using CAD, dispatchers can record details about the incident. These include the vehicles and personnel dispatched. Dispatchers also use CAD to track the status of emergency responders in real time. CAD's automation of various tasks allows dispatchers to address emergencies with efficiency. It also helps responders arrive at the scene faster.

NEXT GENERATION 911

Dispatchers in some parts of the United States use Next Generation 911, or NG911. This is a digital, internet-based system. It allows for multimedia communication between the

public and dispatchers. With NG911, dispatchers can receive photos, videos, and text messages in addition to phone calls. The ability to share media is essential in situations where speaking is hard or impossible. Most states have either implemented NG911 or are in the process of implementing it.

MEDICAL RESPONDERS

PPE

Personal protective equipment, or PPE, is an essential tool for workers responding to a medical emergency. Medical responders often wear gloves, gowns, face masks, and face shields. These help them avoid exposure to hazardous germs and bodily fluids. PPE also protects the patients responders care for. Other protective equipment worn by responders includes helmets, knee pads, and goggles.

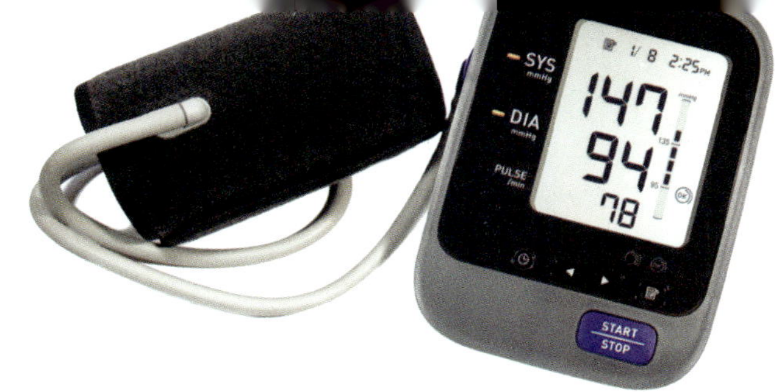

BASIC BODY FUNCTION TESTING TOOLS

EMS specialists use various tools to quickly assess a patient's physical state. They use a thermometer to take a patient's temperature. And a stethoscope is used to listen to their heart and lungs. A blood pressure monitor measures how forcefully blood pushes against the walls of the blood vessels.

Responders may also use a pulse oximeter or a blood glucose meter. A pulse oximeter attaches to a patient's finger. It uses light to measure the amount of oxygen in the blood. A blood glucose meter measures the amount of sugar in the blood. The responder pricks the patient's finger to get a small blood sample. They use a test strip to gather the blood. The test strip is then inserted into the meter, which displays the result on a screen.

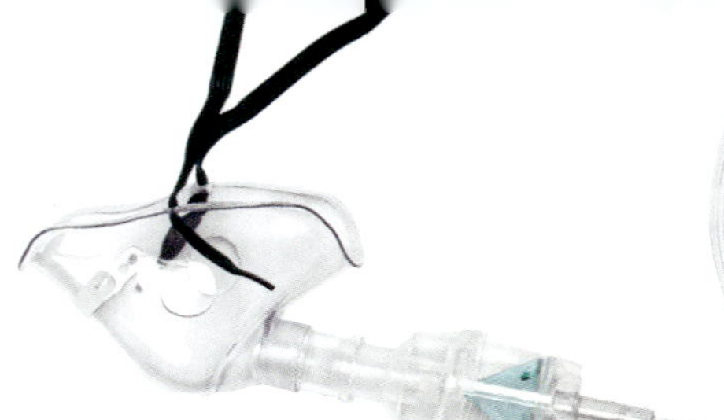

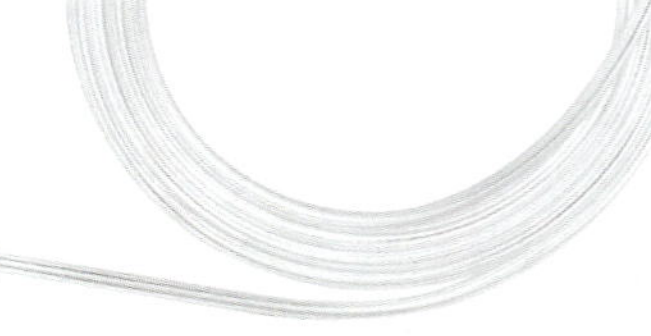

WOUND CARE

Injured patients often need wound care. Responders may use saline solution to clean a wound. Soft cloth called dressing is used to cover the wound and absorb blood. Then a bandage holds the dressing in place. Sometimes, responders must use adhesives, staples, or sutures to close wounds. If an injury results in uncontrolled bleeding, a responder may use a tourniquet. This is a band that is wrapped tightly above the wound. It stops the flow of blood to the wound until the wound can be closed.

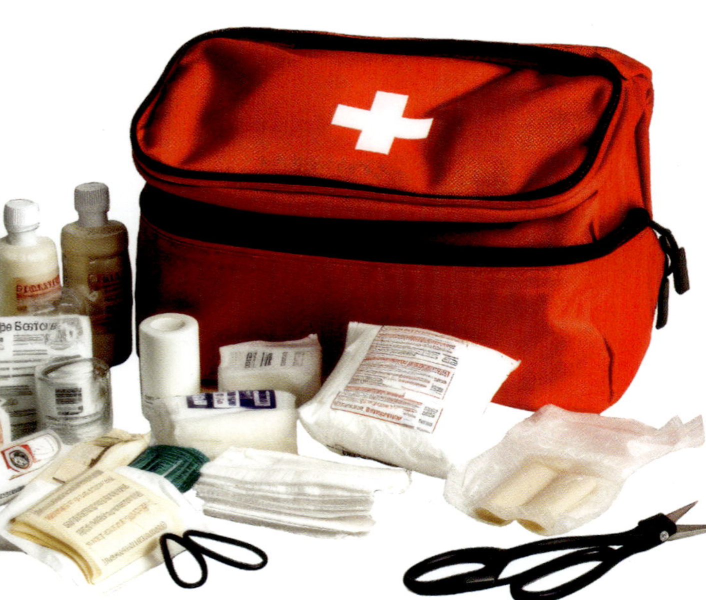

BREATHING DEVICES

If a patient is having trouble breathing, a responder may supply them with oxygen. This can be done through a mask placed over the mouth. Responders may also place tubes into the patient's nose to provide oxygen.

If a patient has fluid in their airway, responders may use a device called a suction unit, or aspirator. The device has a tube attached to a machine. It works like a vacuum to suck the fluid out through a patient's nose or mouth. Responders may also use curved tubes called airway adjuncts. These help to keep the patient's airway open. In some cases, medical personnel use ventilators to move air in and out of a patient's lungs. Ventilators are machines or handheld devices with tubes that connect to a patient's breathing tubes or oxygen mask.

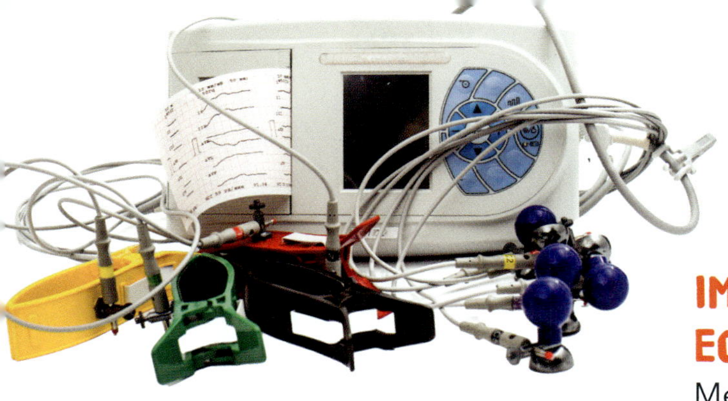

ECG MACHINE

ECG stands for electrocardiogram. An ECG machine is used to monitor the electrical signals that make a patient's heart pump. Medical workers may use this machine to understand the cause of symptoms such as chest pain, shortness of breath, or irregular heartbeats.

DEFIBRILLATOR

EMS specialists use a device called a defibrillator if a patient's heart is beating abnormally or not beating at all. A defibrillator has paddles or sticky pads. A responder places these on the patient's chest. The defibrillator then delivers an electric shock to the patient's heart through the paddles or pads. This shock is intended to restart the heart at a normal rhythm.

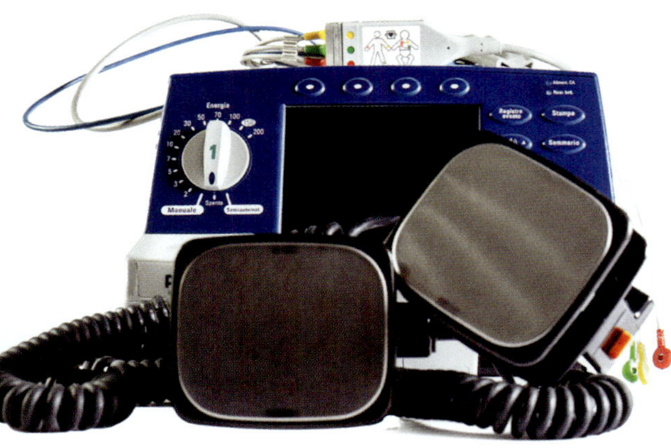

IMMOBILIZATION EQUIPMENT

Medical responders use various tools and devices to immobilize injured parts of the body. These prevent movement that can cause further injury. One kind of immobilizing tool is a splint. This rigid device is used to support broken bones, sprained ankles, and other musculoskeletal injuries. Another immobilizing device is a neck brace, which wraps around a patient's neck. It supports the upper spine and limits head movement. Responders also use spinal boards. These rigid, full-body supports are used to immobilize the entire body.

IVS & INFUSION PUMPS

Medical responders often administer medicine or nutrients to a patient using an intravenous line, or IV. This flexible tube is placed into a patient's vein with the help of a needle. Fluids then flow from a bag through the tube into the vein. Sometimes, IVs are connected to infusion pumps. These devices deliver the fluids in precise amounts at a controlled rate.

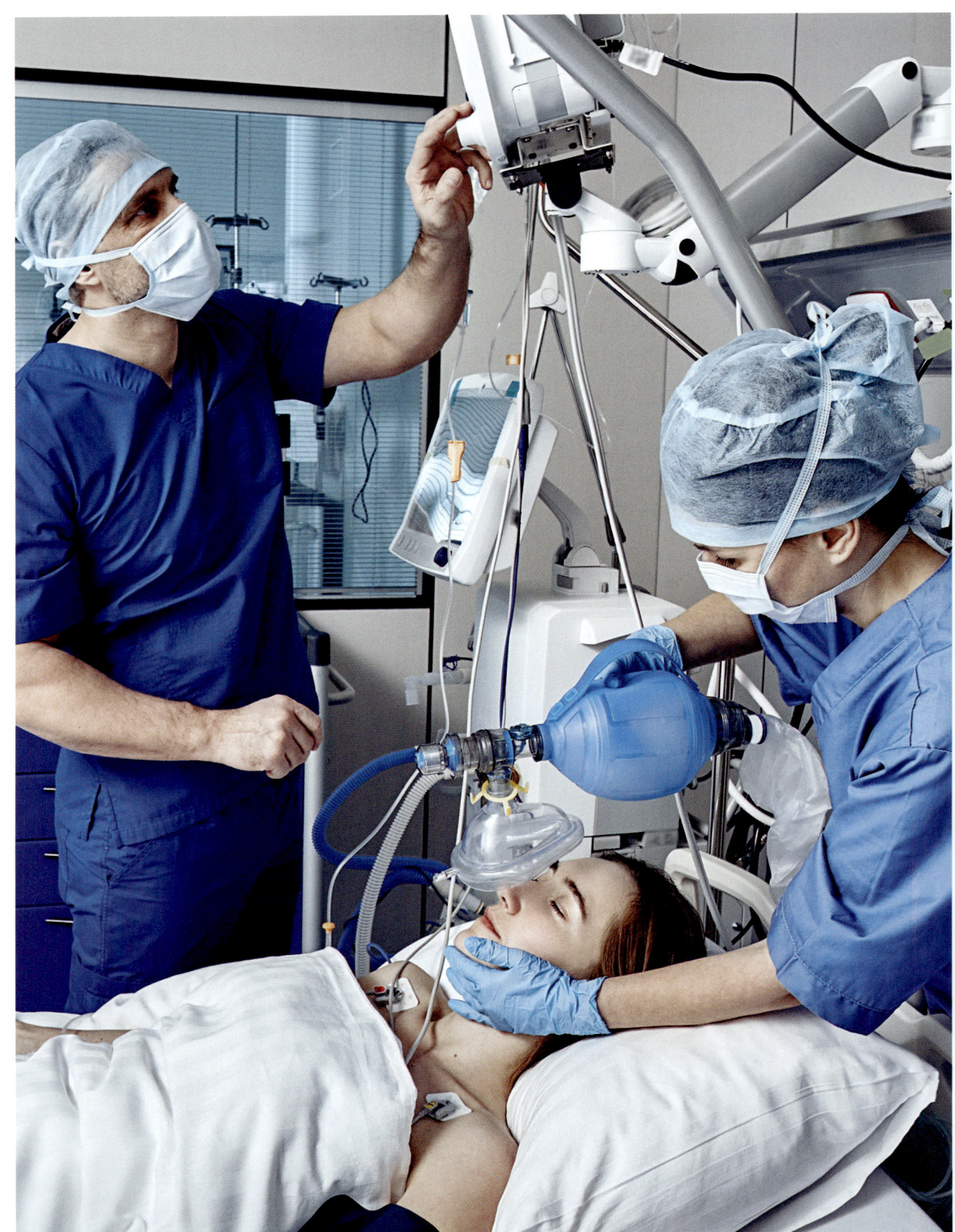

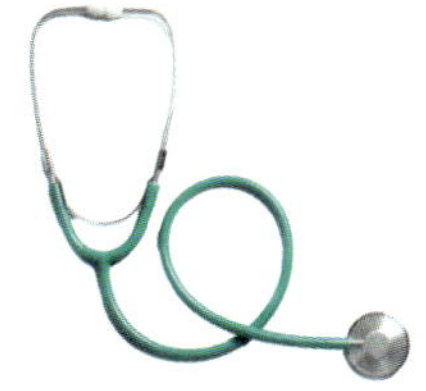

SPECIAL SKILLS

Explore some of the skills that EMS specialists need to do their jobs.

CALM UNDER PRESSURE

In life-threatening situations, quick action is essential. However, rushing can lead to mistakes. That's why emergency dispatchers and responders must maintain their focus and awareness as they make quick decisions. And when callers and patients are panicked, EMS specialists must remain calm.

COMMUNICATION

Dispatchers provide instructions to 911 callers and emergency responders. ER technicians follow instructions from nurses and doctors. Community paramedics discuss health matters with a diverse range of patients. All these tasks require the ability to communicate with clarity.

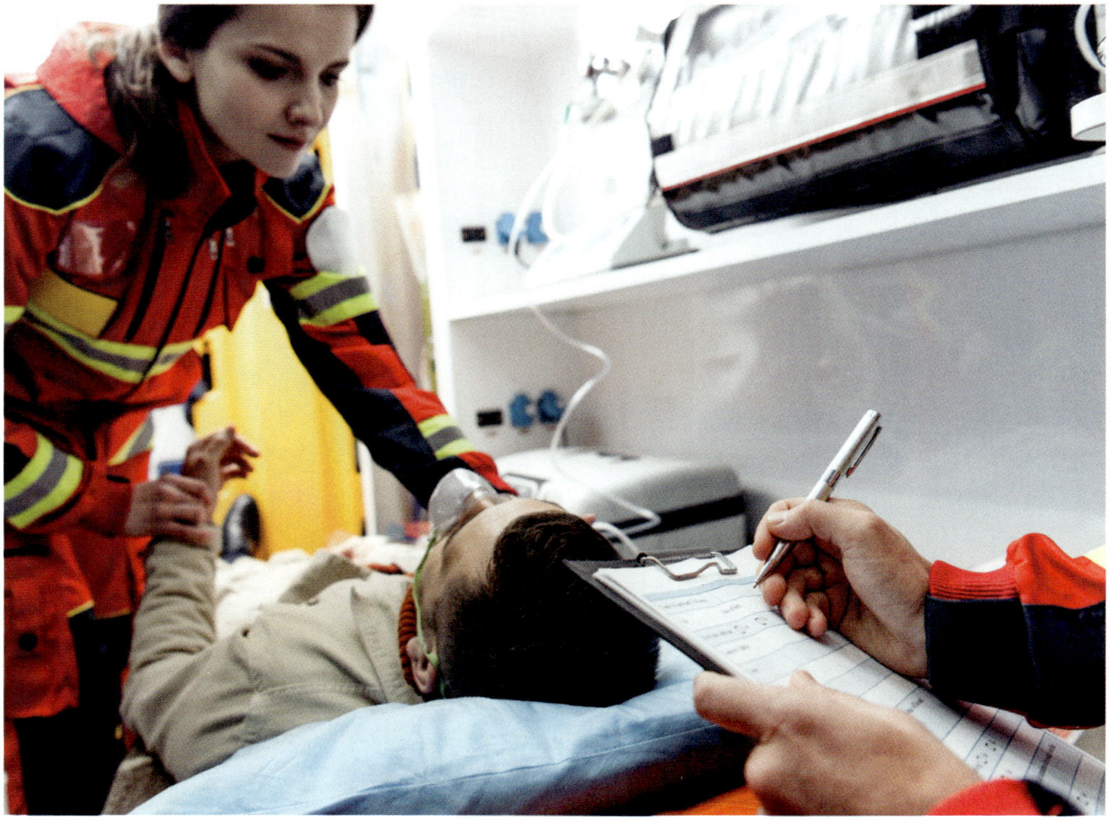

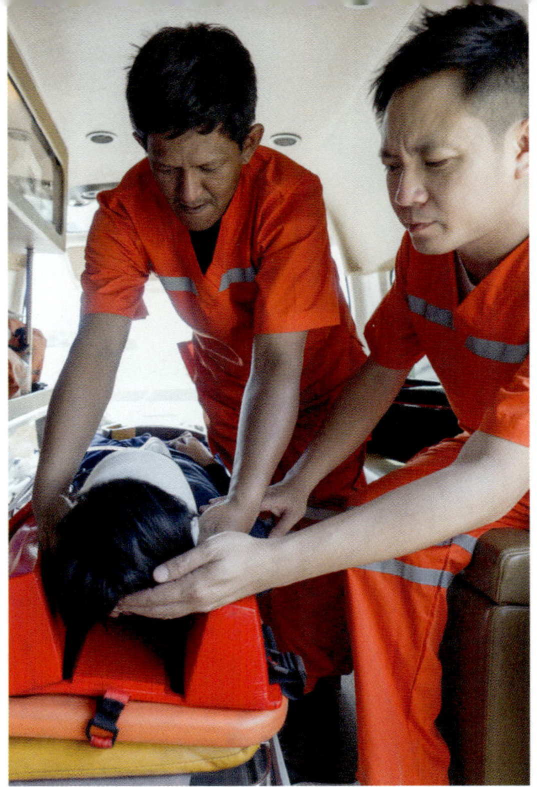

RESILIENCE

Emergency dispatchers and responders encounter highly distressing situations on a regular basis. If they hold on to the stress of an emergency, they won't be able to effectively respond to the next one. This means EMS specialists must have resilience. This is the ability to recover quickly from mental or physical strain.

COMPASSION

Emergency responders often risk their own well-being to help complete strangers. This is difficult to do without a strong sense of compassion for all people. EMS specialists see every patient as deserving of kindness and care.

STAMINA

Emergency responders need physical stamina to run, kneel on the ground, lift patients, and more throughout a single shift. Meanwhile, dispatchers must maintain their energy and focus as they handle one emergency call after the next. This takes great mental stamina.

FLEXIBILITY

Emergencies can happen at any time of day, on any day of the year. That means EMS specialists must work shifts at night and on weekends and holidays. Overnight shifts can be especially hard on emergency workers, as this is when the body naturally wants to rest. In some cases, responders can nap between calls. But they must be prepared to spring into action at a moment's notice.

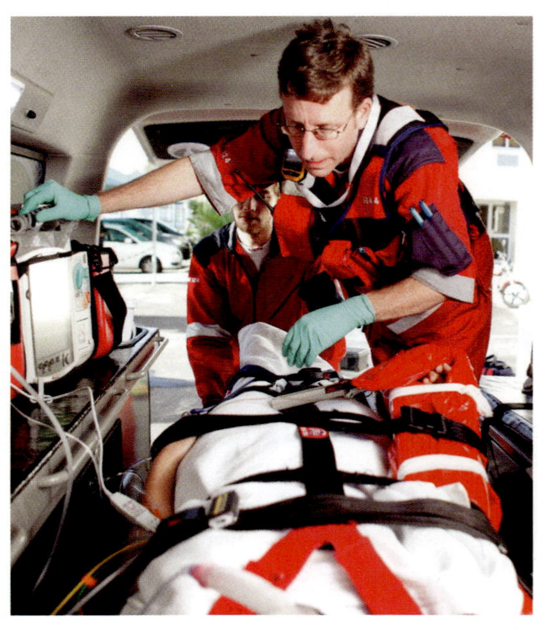

TEAMWORK

Dispatchers and responders coordinate with one another to help patients dealing with medical emergencies. ER technicians work with hospital nurses and doctors. And community paramedics collaborate with other health care providers to meet their patients' needs. Saving lives is a team effort.

TECHNICAL SKILLS

Responding to emergencies quickly and effectively requires advanced tools and technology. EMS specialists must be able to operate devices such as a dispatcher's CAD software or a responder's defibrillator. EMS specialists need technical skills and knowledge to do this work.

CAREERS IN EMS

EMS specialists work in a variety of roles. They do their jobs in call centers, ambulances, hospitals, and even patients' homes. Though their job titles vary, they all work to save lives and maintain the health of their communities.

EMERGENCY DISPATCHER

When there's an emergency, what number do you call? 911! That call goes through to an emergency dispatcher. Many dispatchers work in communication centers known as public safety answering points. There, they answer 911 calls and dispatch emergency services to respond to those calls. Dispatchers can also work for police and fire departments, ambulance services, and hospitals.

ANSWER & ASSESS

When a dispatcher answers a call, their job is to collect essential information from the caller. This includes the nature and location of the emergency. This can be difficult when the caller is panicked and struggling to communicate clearly. Additionally, sometimes callers don't know where they are or can't provide an exact address.

The dispatcher must speak calmly and clearly as they ask the caller questions. They must also be familiar with major streets,

highways, and landmarks in the area. This is important so they can determine the caller's exact location. As the dispatcher gathers information, they must make quick decisions. If they are handling multiple emergency calls, they must prioritize the ones that require the quickest response.

DIRECT & DISPATCH

Based on the details of the emergency, the dispatcher connects with the appropriate responders. This may be police, firefighters, ambulance services, or a combination of personnel. The dispatcher relays the information they gathered from the caller. They also provide clear instructions for the responders. Then the dispatcher tracks the status of the responders, often while remaining on the line with the caller.

ADVISE & ASSIST

Until responders arrive at the scene of an emergency, the dispatcher does everything they can to assist those waiting for help. Sometimes they provide medical guidance over the phone. This can be instructions on how to perform basic first aid procedures. Other times, they advise callers on how to remain safe while waiting for help. The guidance of an emergency dispatcher can help save lives!

EMS unit for the 2022 Boston Marathon. EMS may work with large events to provide better and faster emergency medical care to event participants.

Dispatchers can be notified of emergencies through various sources. These include text messages, social media posts, and alarm systems.

EMTs work alongside other emergency professionals depending on the type of emergency. For example, they work with firefighters and police if there is a vehicle accident.

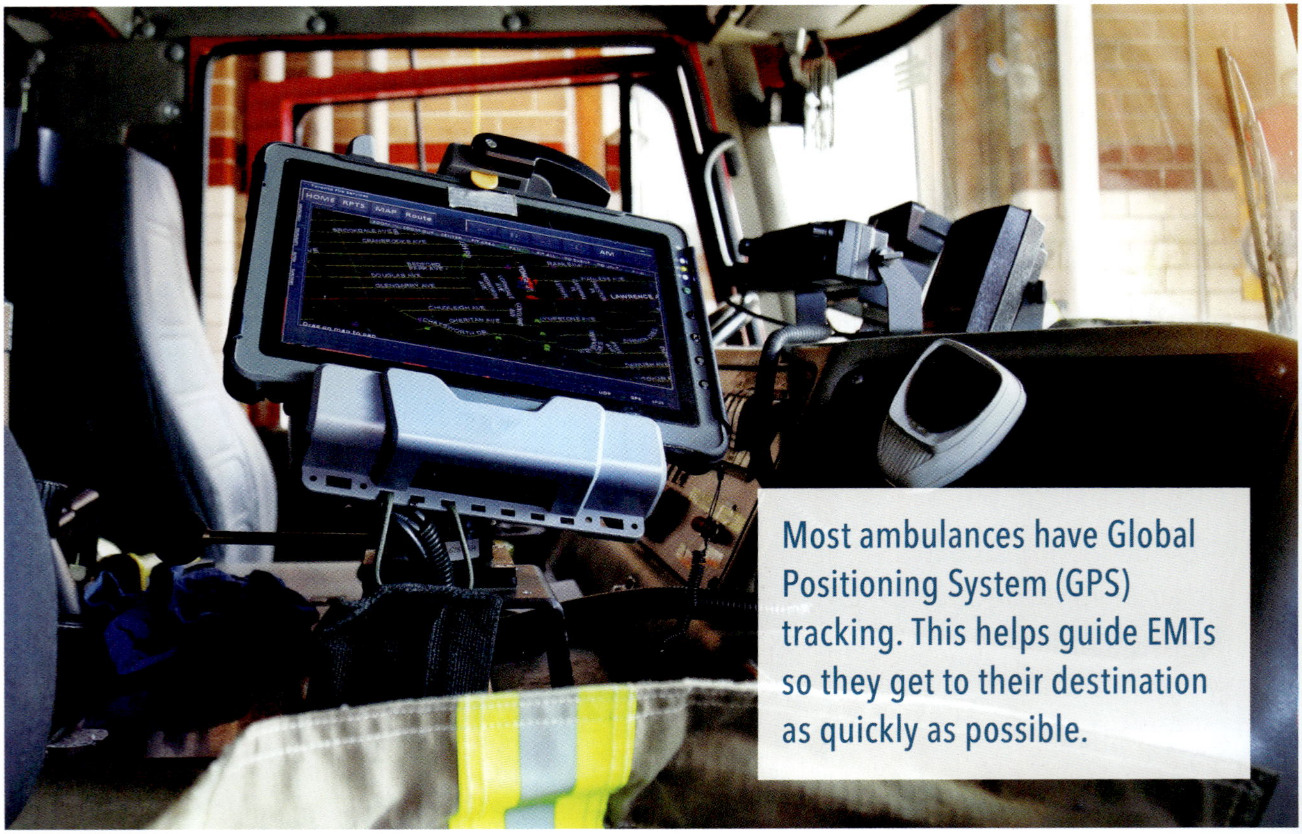

Most ambulances have Global Positioning System (GPS) tracking. This helps guide EMTs so they get to their destination as quickly as possible.

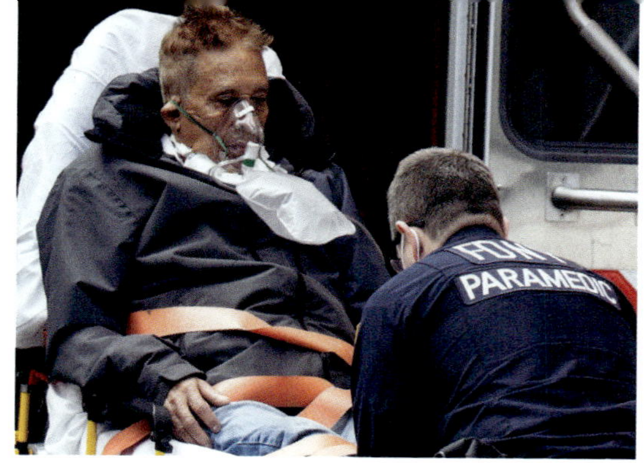

EMERGENCY MEDICAL TECHNICIAN

Among the first responders to a medical emergency is an emergency medical technician (EMT). Most EMTs work for ambulance services or hospitals. They are trained to provide lifesaving care to patients. They also safely transport patients to the hospital in an ambulance.

RESPOND & ASSESS

When EMTs are dispatched, they determine the quickest route to their destination. Driving an ambulance to an emergency requires focus and sharp awareness of surrounding traffic. Ambulance drivers can typically travel faster than the posted speed limit. But they must do so with great caution to ensure the safety of others sharing the road. Once EMTs arrive at their destination, they quickly assess the severity of a patient's illness or injury. This helps them determine what kind of care to provide.

AIRWAY MANAGEMENT

If a patient is struggling to breathe or not breathing at all, EMTs take steps to open the patient's airway and deliver oxygen to their lungs. A basic technique to open the airway is to tilt the patient's head back and lift their chin. In some cases, an EMT may perform abdominal thrusts to remove an obstruction, such as food, from the airway. In other cases, they insert a tube into the patient's throat or nose. EMTs also use ventilation devices to deliver oxygen into patients' lungs.

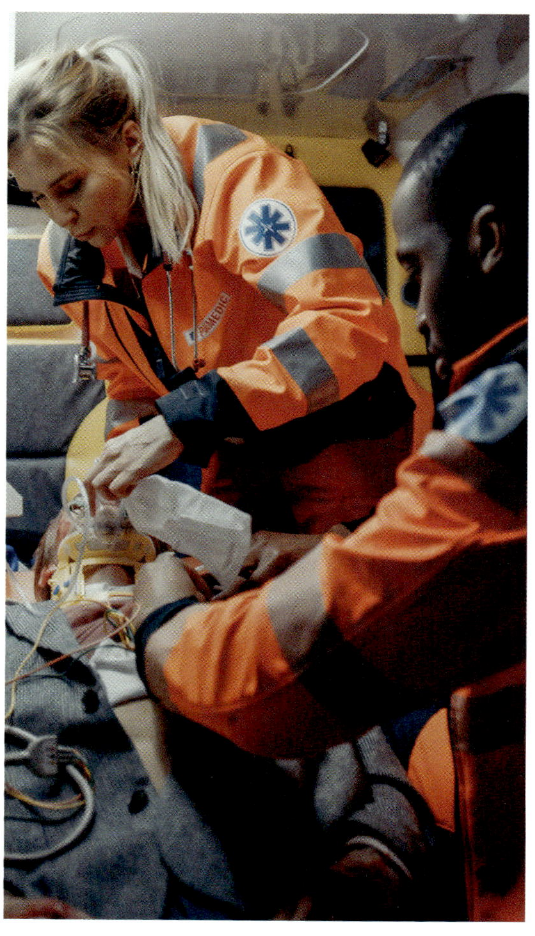

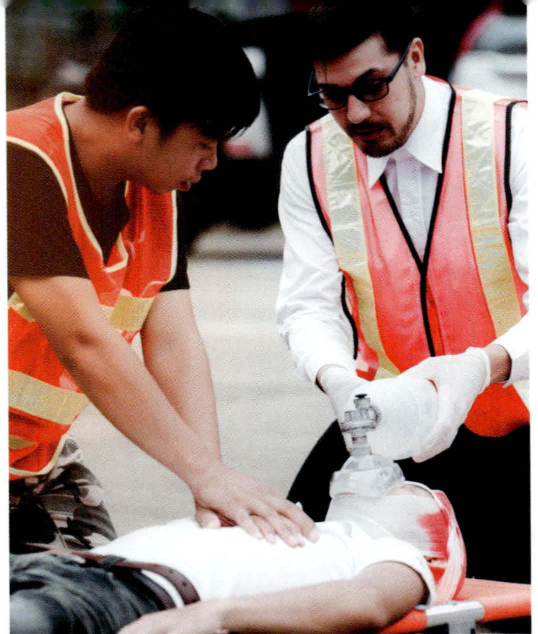

CPR & DEFIBRILLATION

EMTs may encounter a patient in cardiac arrest. This means the patient's heart is not pumping blood. Because the blood delivers oxygen to the body's organs, cardiac arrest deprives the body of oxygen. This can quickly lead to death.

An EMT immediately responds to cardiac arrest by performing cardiopulmonary resuscitation, or CPR. CPR involves pressing down on the patient's chest and blowing air into their mouth. This keeps blood flowing to the patient's organs. EMTs typically use this technique while they prepare a defibrillator. This device helps restore the heart's normal rhythm. Unless they have advanced training, EMTs typically use automatic defibrillators. These do the work of determining how powerful a shock to deliver to a patient's heart.

WOUND CARE

EMTs are prepared to treat all kinds of wounds. These can be anything from burns to cuts. For many wounds, EMTs clean the area and apply dressings and bandages. They may also apply an analgesic to relieve pain. If a patient's wound has resulted in severe bleeding, an EMT may use their hand to apply direct pressure to the wound to stop the bleeding. Other techniques that control bleeding include filling the wound with dressings and applying a tourniquet.

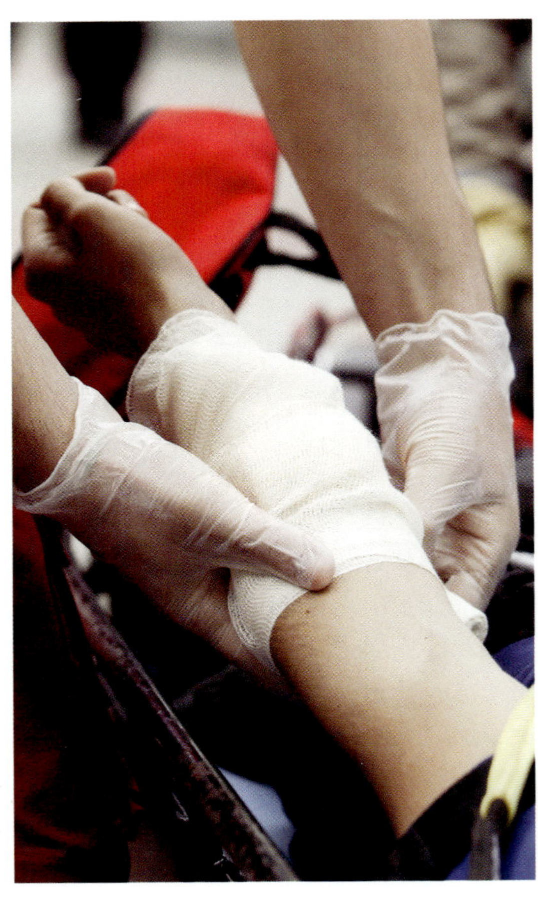

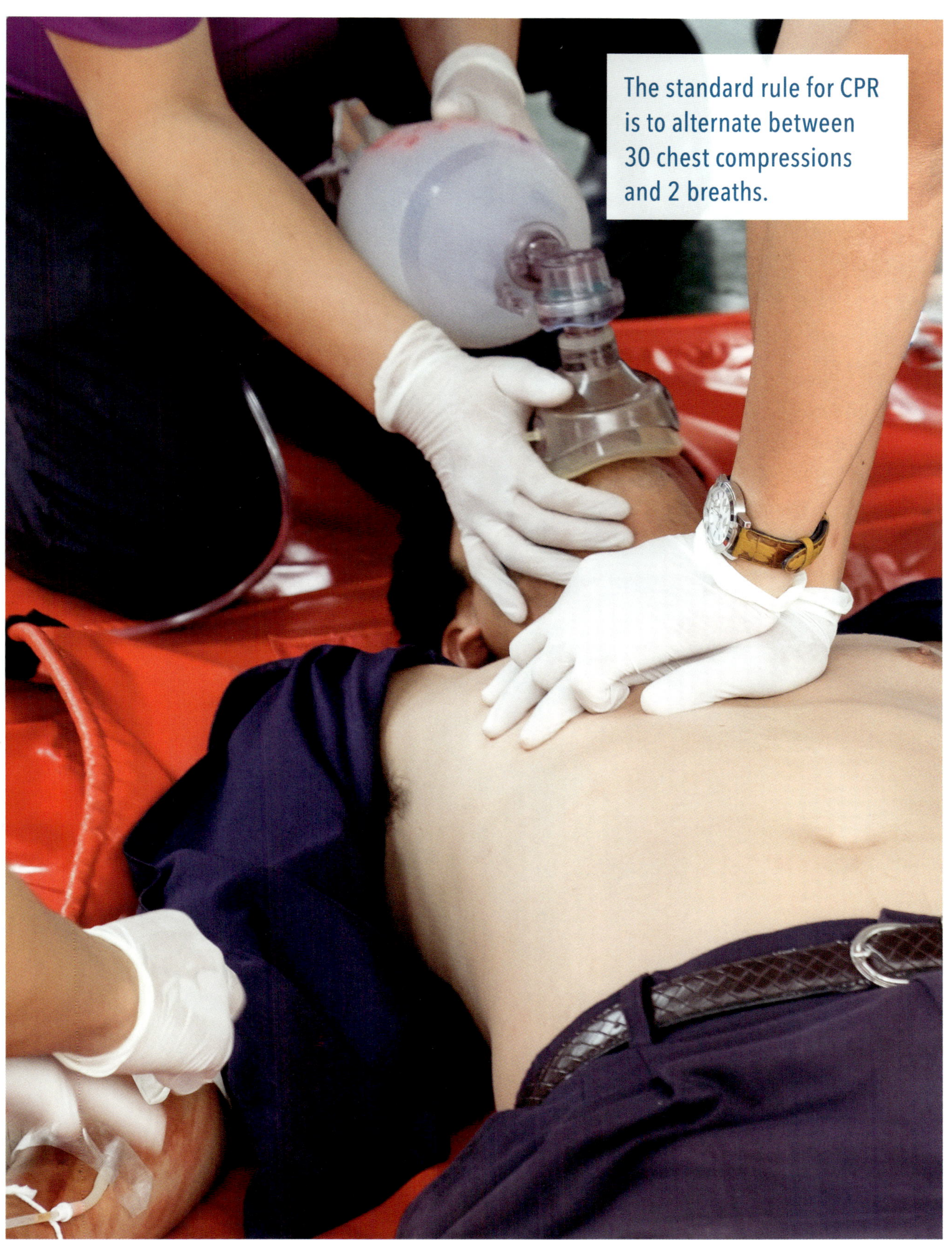

The standard rule for CPR is to alternate between 30 chest compressions and 2 breaths.

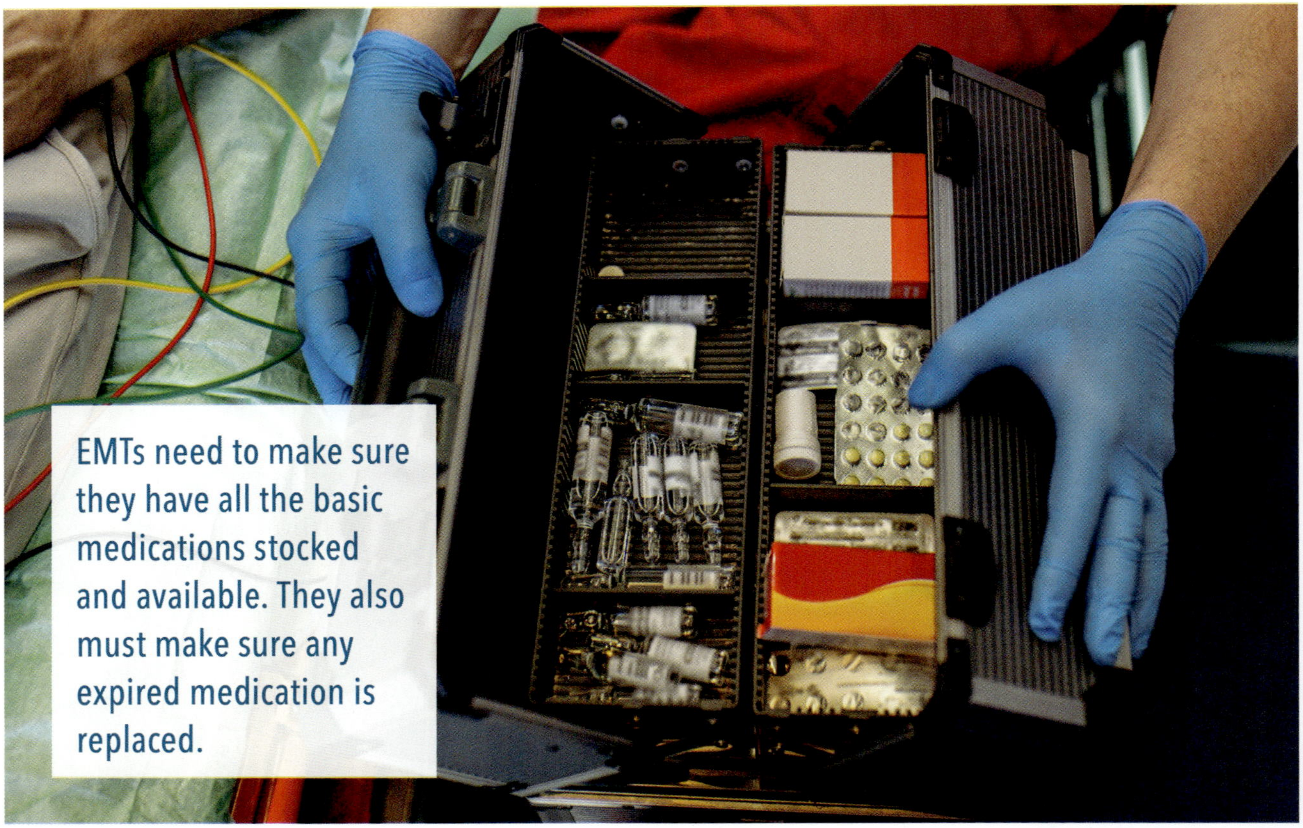

EMTs need to make sure they have all the basic medications stocked and available. They also must make sure any expired medication is replaced.

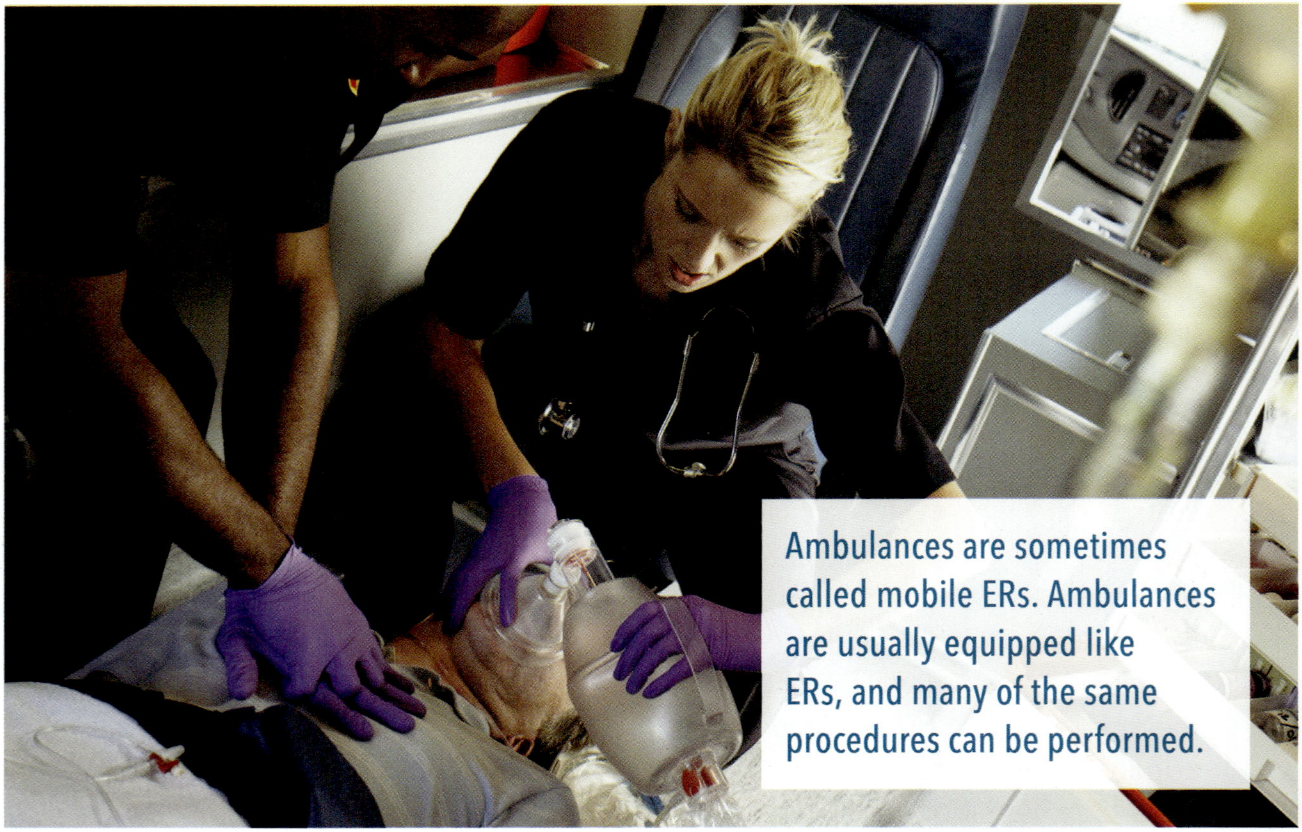

Ambulances are sometimes called mobile ERs. Ambulances are usually equipped like ERs, and many of the same procedures can be performed.

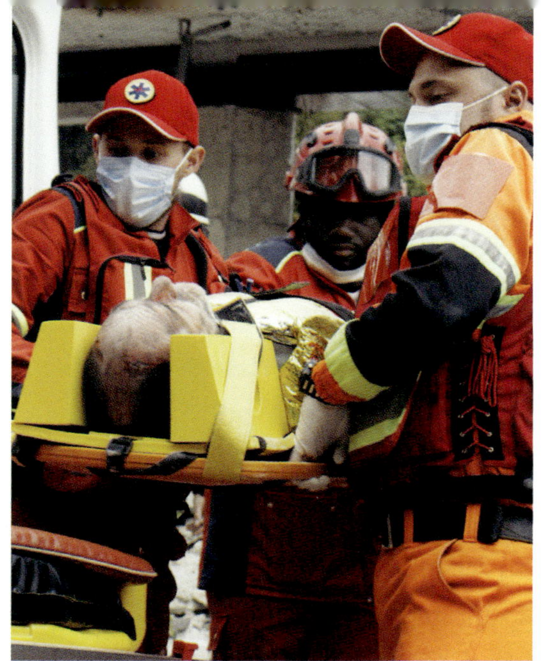

IMMOBILIZATION

If a patient has a broken bone, an EMT uses a splint. This both immobilizes and protects the injured area. EMTs may use a spinal board or neck brace if they suspect a patient has injured their spine. This is to prevent fractured vertebrae from damaging the spinal cord, which can lead to paralysis.

MEDICINE

Sometimes EMTs administer medications to patients. For example, an EMT may give aspirin to a patient to help prevent blood clots. An EMT might also administer epinephrine to a patient having a severe allergic reaction. And they may give glucose to a patient with low blood sugar. The specific medications an EMT is allowed to administer are determined by the state they work in.

PATIENT TRANSPORT

If a patient needs to go to the hospital, EMTs must carefully transfer the patient onto a gurney. They secure the patient to the gurney with multiple straps. Then they lift the gurney onto the ambulance and secure it to the inside of the vehicle. During transport, EMTs continue to monitor the patient and provide any necessary medical care.

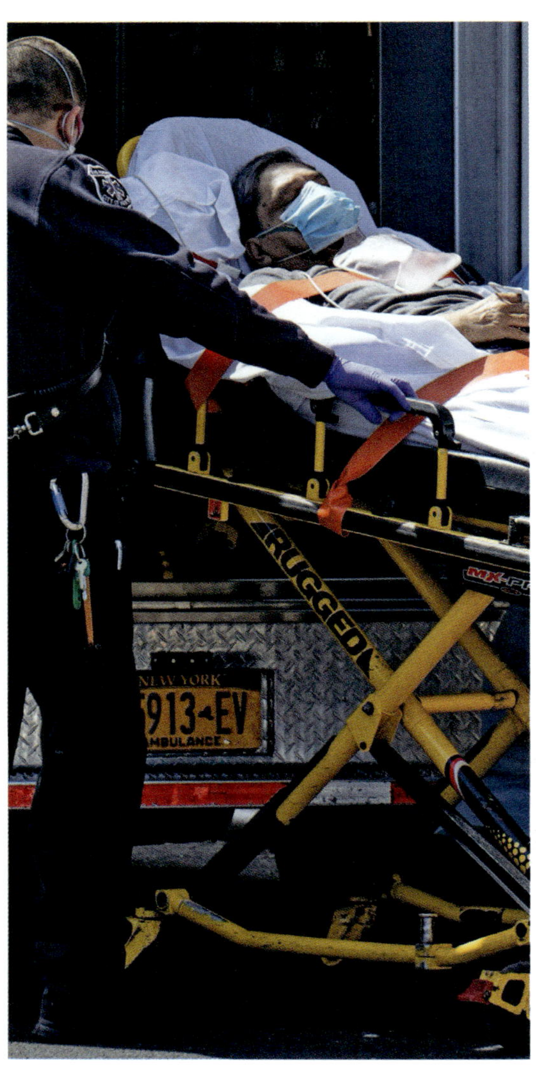

CLEANING & MAINTENANCE

After responding to a call, EMTs must make sure they are ready for the next one. They are responsible for disinfecting used equipment and restocking supplies. They also clean the interior and exterior of the ambulance. Then they make sure the vehicle is in proper working order.

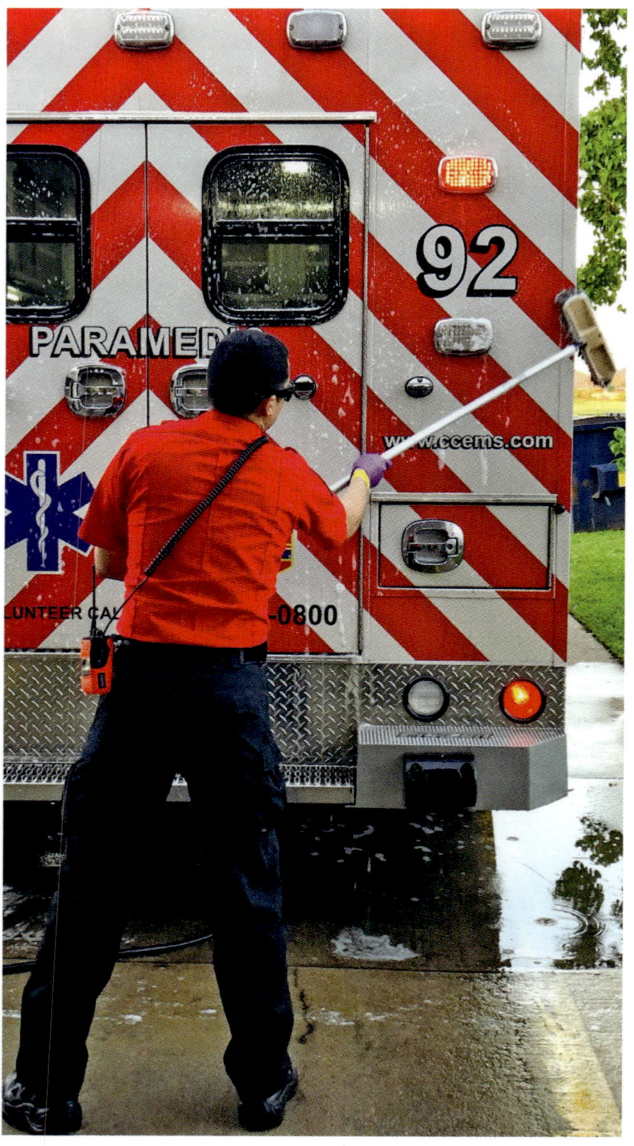

PARAMEDIC

Paramedics often work alongside EMTs and provide all the same services as EMTs. However, paramedics receive more extensive training. They are therefore qualified to perform more advanced procedures. These procedures are more challenging to execute and can harm a patient if performed improperly.

ADVANCED AIRWAY MANAGEMENT

A paramedic can perform more complicated procedures to open a patient's airway. One of these procedures is called endotracheal intubation. In this process, a paramedic inserts a long tube past the patient's throat and into their trachea. Then they inflate a small balloon attached to the tube to secure it in place. The tube can now deliver oxygen into the patient's lungs!

ELECTROCARDIOGRAMS

Paramedics often encounter patients who are experiencing chest pain, weakness, or shortness of breath. These can be signs of serious heart problems. To determine the cause of these symptoms, a paramedic may

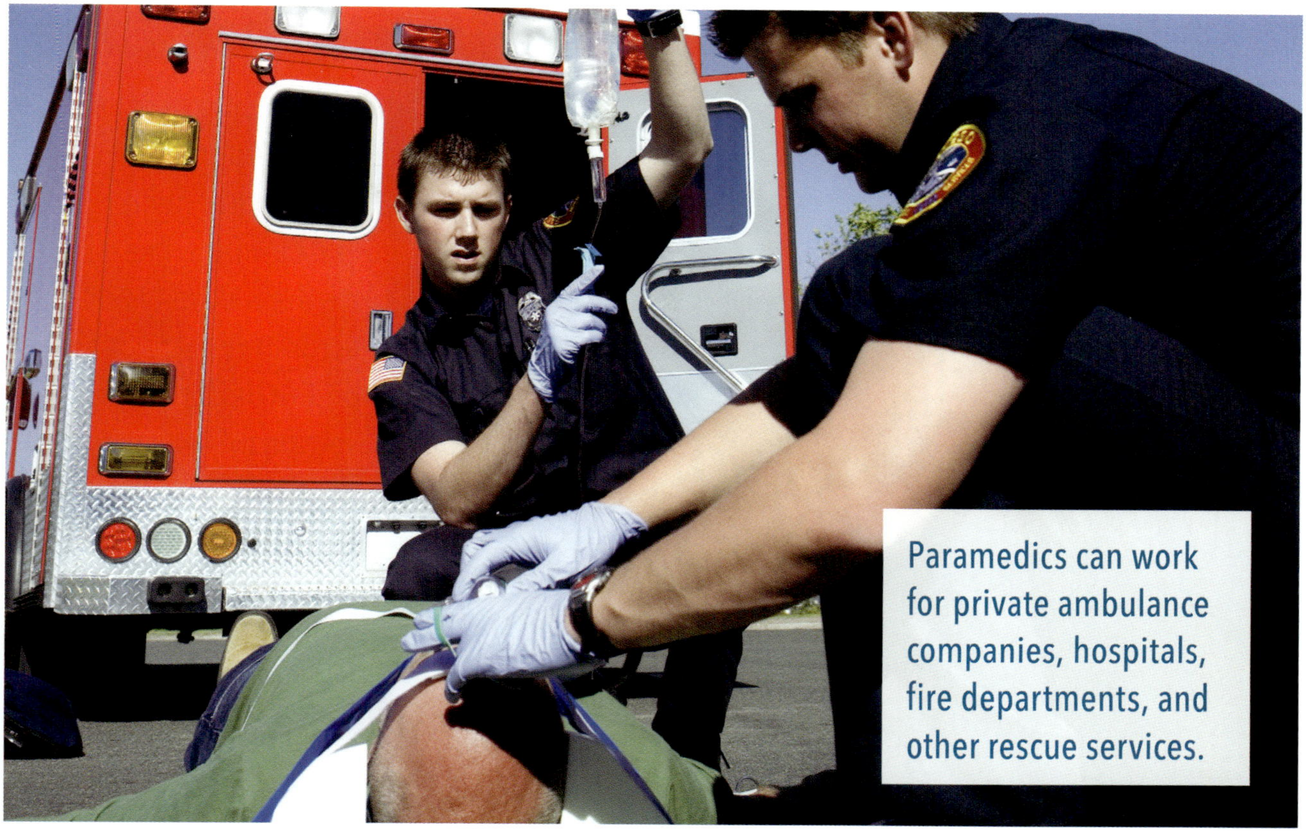

Paramedics can work for private ambulance companies, hospitals, fire departments, and other rescue services.

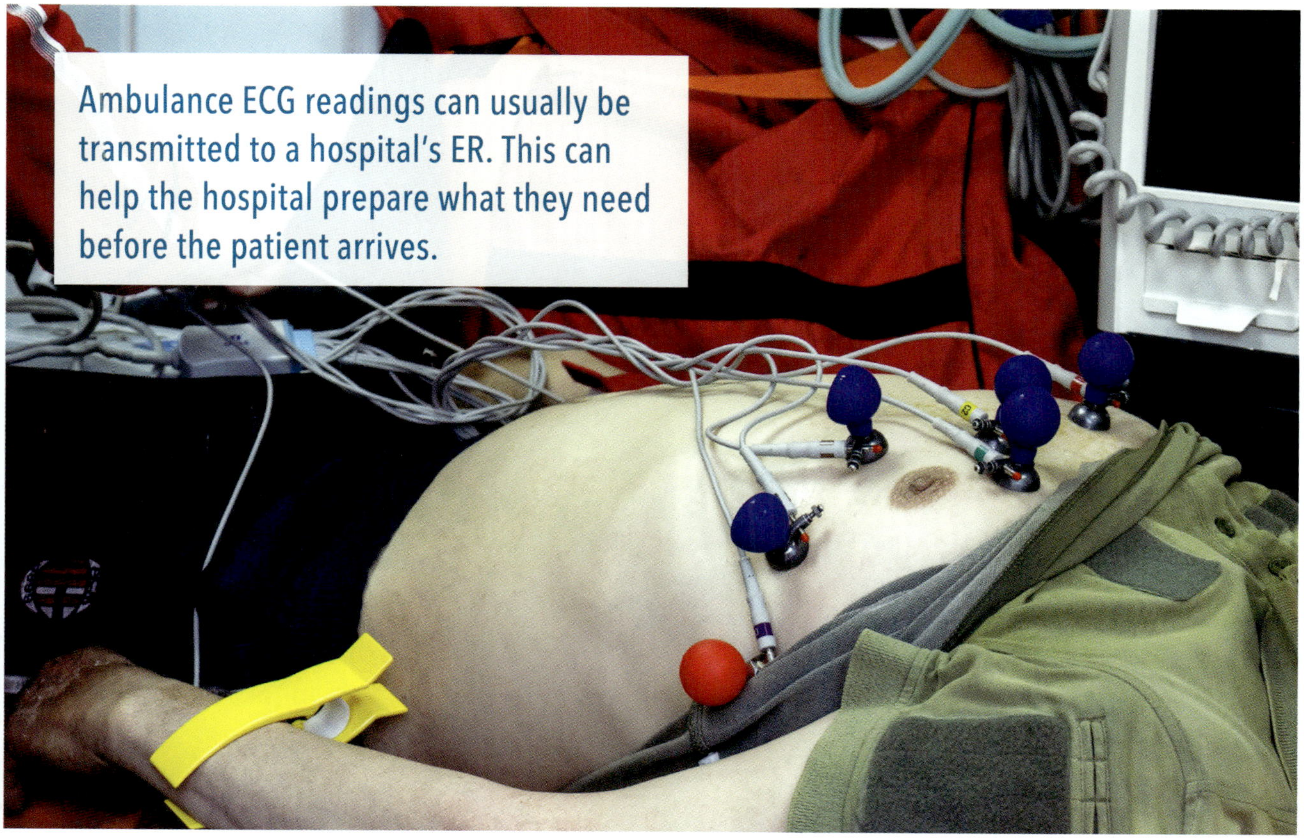

Ambulance ECG readings can usually be transmitted to a hospital's ER. This can help the hospital prepare what they need before the patient arrives.

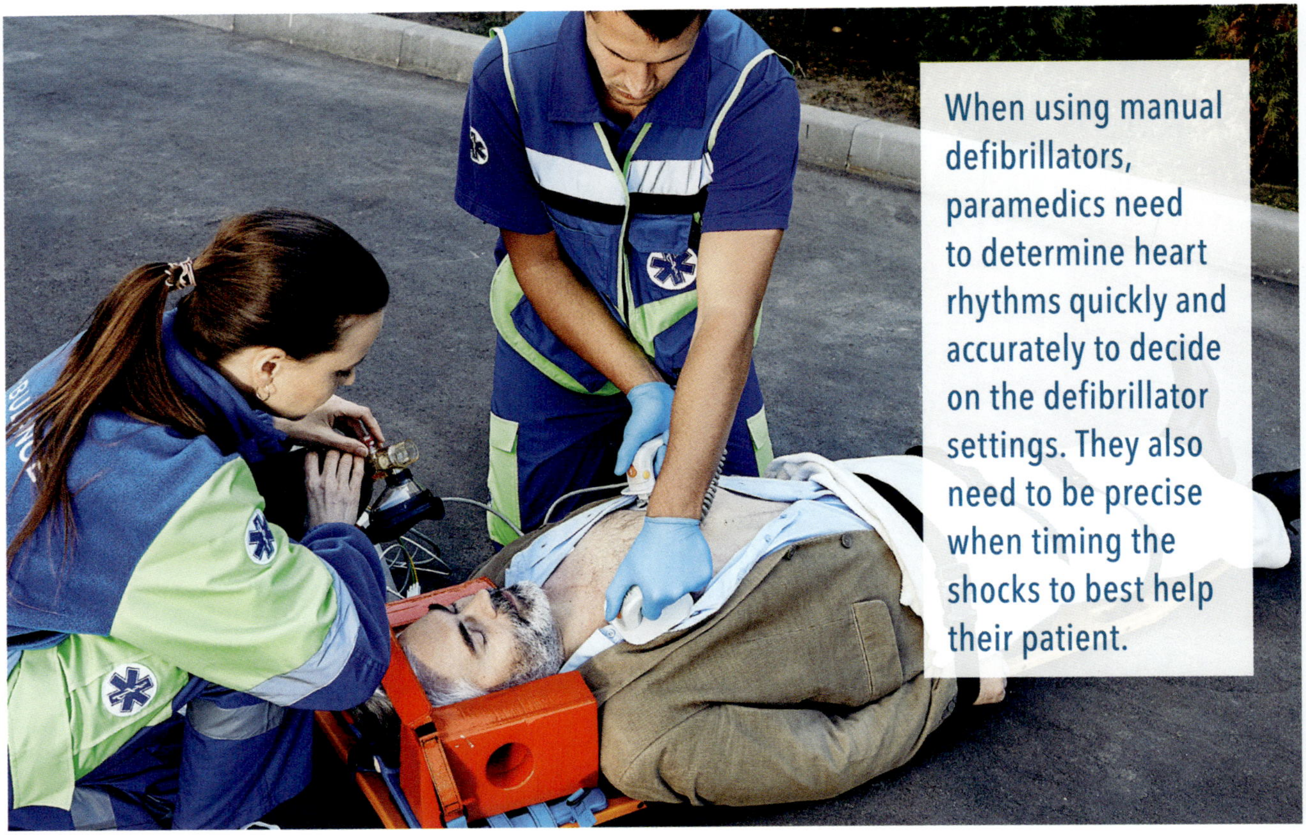

When using manual defibrillators, paramedics need to determine heart rhythms quickly and accurately to decide on the defibrillator settings. They also need to be precise when timing the shocks to best help their patient.

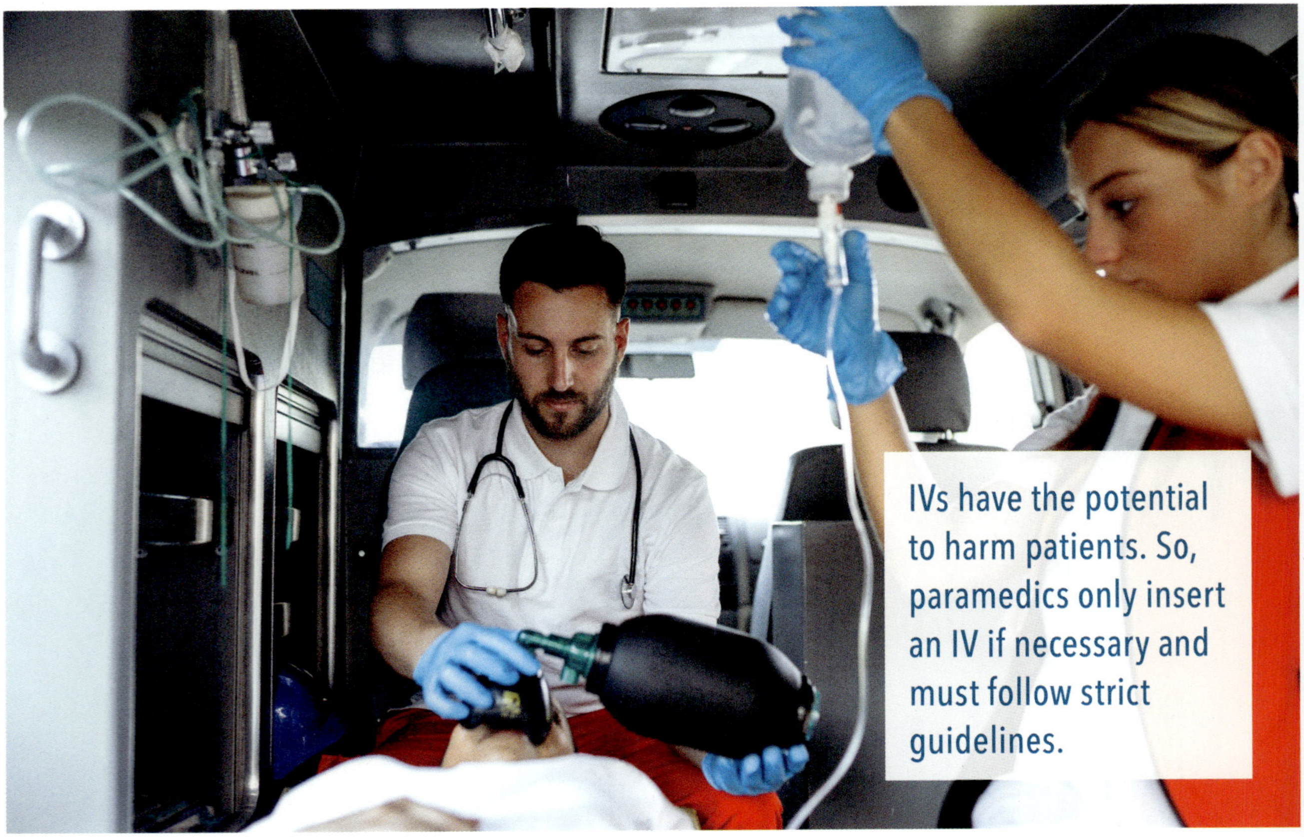

IVs have the potential to harm patients. So, paramedics only insert an IV if necessary and must follow strict guidelines.

conduct an ECG. For this test, a paramedic attaches sensors to the patient's chest and limbs. Wires connect the sensors to a computer. The computer then records the heart's electrical signals as waves. The paramedic interprets the recording to detect irregular heart rhythms or other heart issues.

MANUAL DEFIBRILLATION

If a patient is in cardiac arrest, a paramedic is trained to use a manual defibrillator. With a manual defibrillator, a paramedic decides how powerful a shock a patient needs. Then they manually adjust the energy level of the shock.

MEDICINE & IVS

Paramedics can administer a wider range of medicines than EMTs. They are also trained to insert IVs. IVs are usually placed in a patient's hand or arm. A paramedic may use an IV to quickly deliver a pain-relieving medication. Or, if a patient is dehydrated, a paramedic may deliver fluids through an IV to rehydrate them.

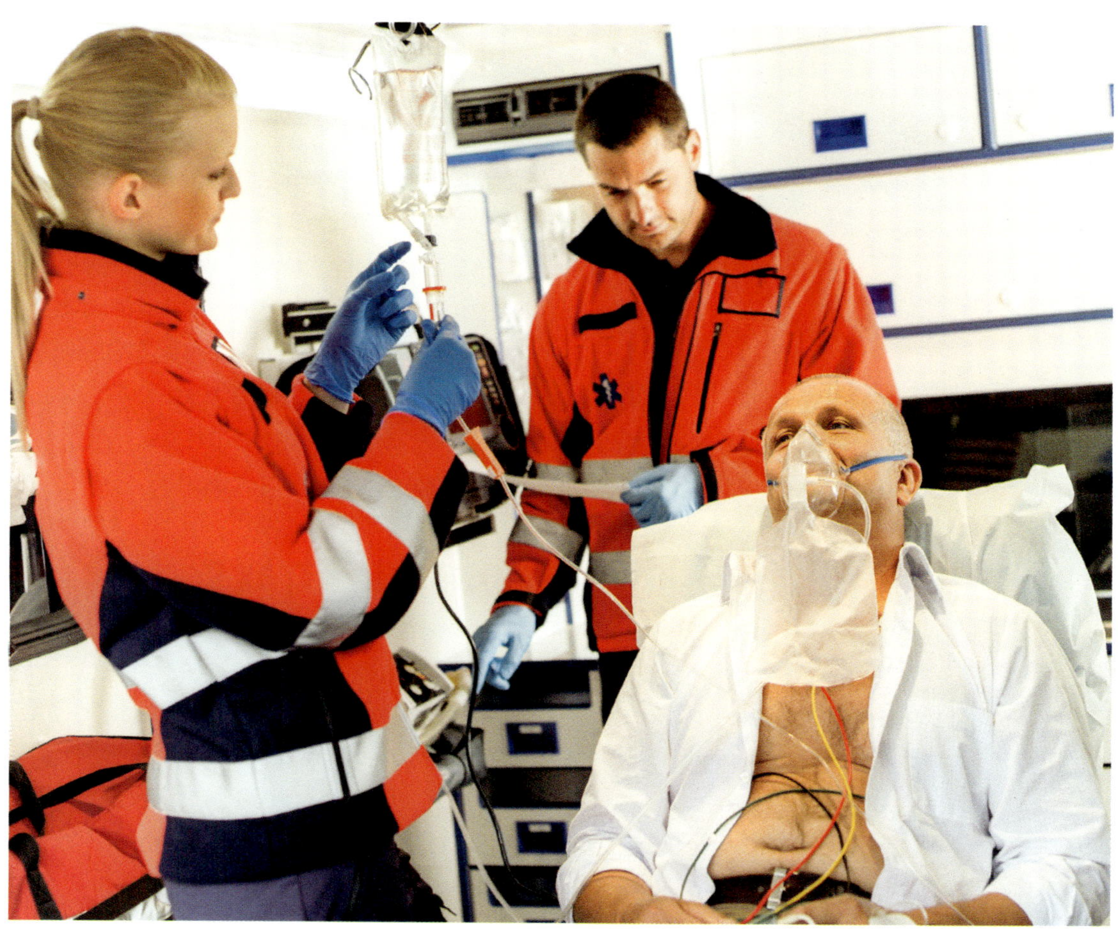

TEAM LEADERSHIP

In addition to providing medical services, a paramedic often leads the other members of their rescue team. They supervise EMTs, make decisions, and give orders. At the same time, a paramedic works under a doctor's supervision. They may communicate with an off-site supervising doctor via phone or radio. Upon arriving at the hospital, the paramedic provides a report of the patient's condition and treatments to the ER staff.

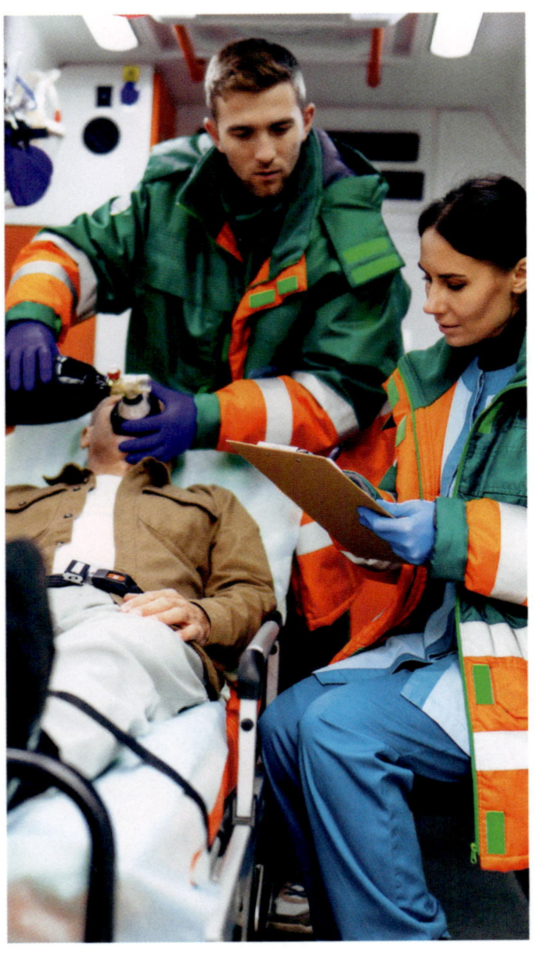

EMERGENCY ROOM TECHNICIAN

When ambulances arrive at a hospital, EMTs and paramedics transfer the care of their patients to ER workers. Among these workers are ER technicians. These specialists assist ER doctors and nurses as they care for sick and injured patients.

INTAKE TO DISCHARGE

An ER tech is responsible for documenting a patient's personal information. This includes their medical history. While the patient is receiving emergency care, the ER tech may provide the patient's family with updates. ER techs also help transfer patients to other areas of the hospital if they need continuing care. After a patient has received emergency care, the ER tech helps discharge them. This includes providing patients with at-home care instructions.

MONITOR VITALS

A patient's vital signs, or vitals, are measurements of their essential body functions. Vitals include pulse rate, temperature, blood pressure, and breathing rate. ER techs help monitor patients' vitals throughout their emergency care.

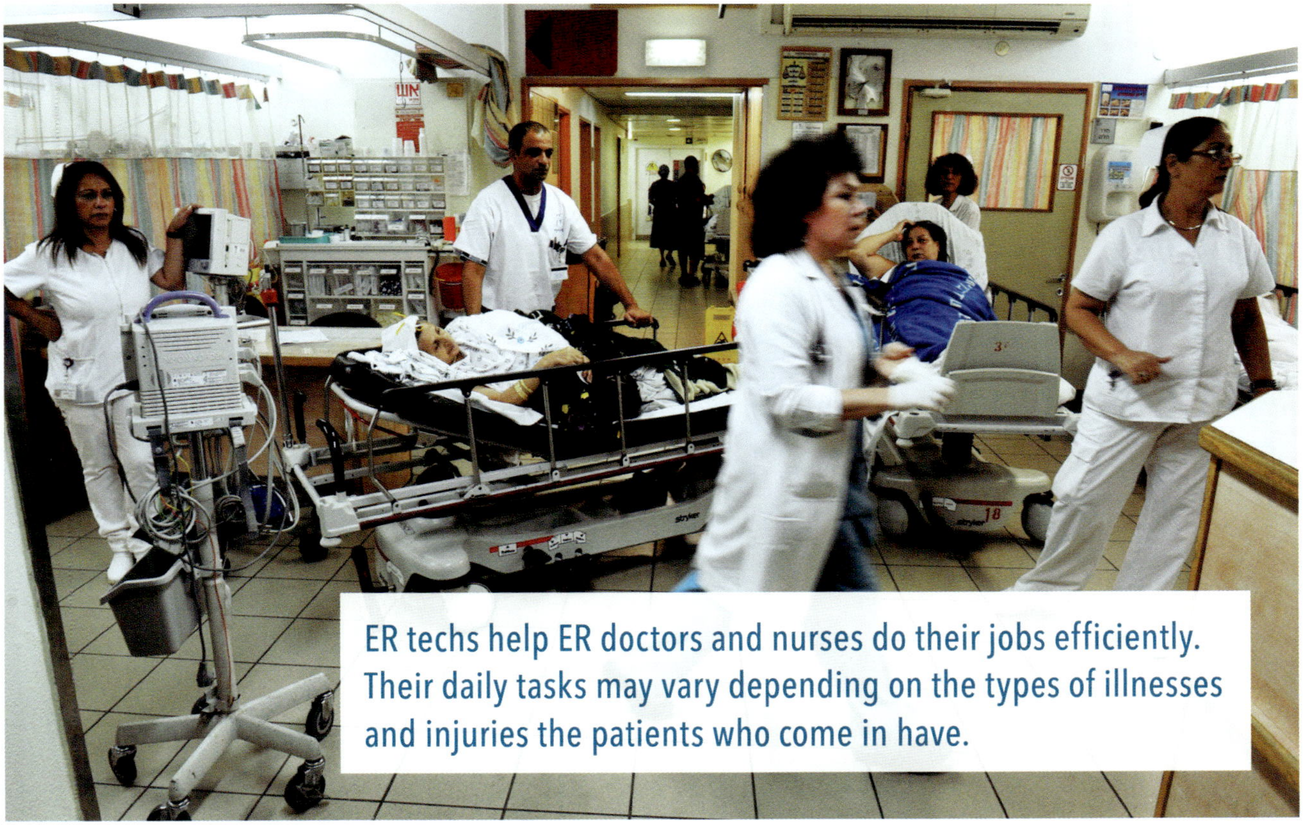

ER techs help ER doctors and nurses do their jobs efficiently. Their daily tasks may vary depending on the types of illnesses and injuries the patients who come in have.

Doctors and nurses use abbreviations when writing notes. ER techs need to be able to understand these when working in the ER.

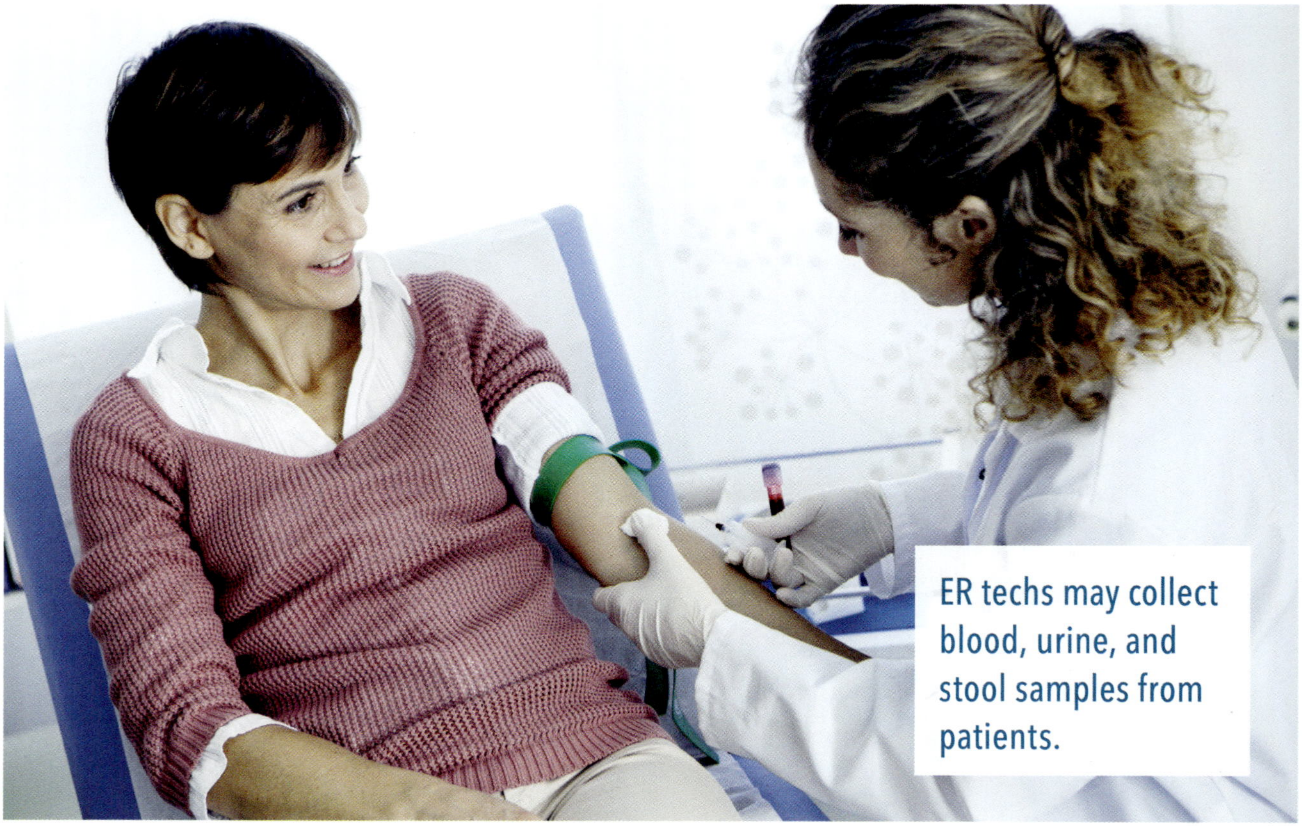

ER techs may collect blood, urine, and stool samples from patients.

ER techs also help instruct patients on how to use mobility aids, such as canes or crutches.

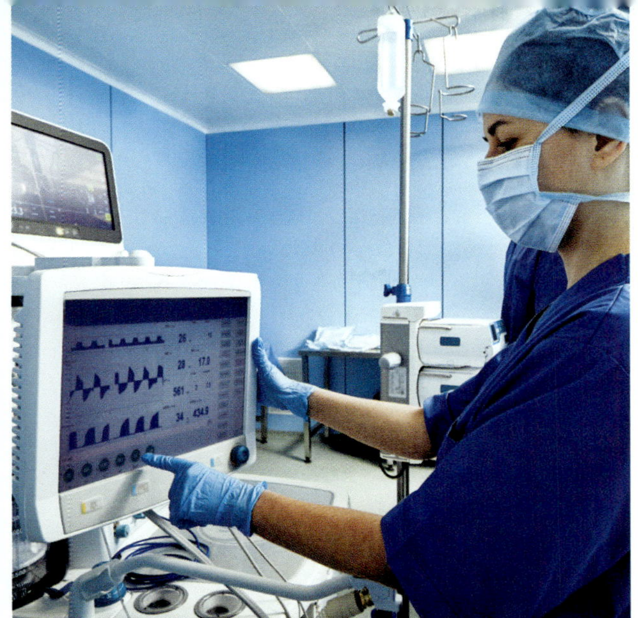

BLOOD DRAWS

Often, ER doctors need blood samples from patients. These help them diagnose or manage a condition. For example, blood samples can indicate issues such as infections, diabetes, heart problems, and more. ER techs are often responsible for collecting blood samples. They also prepare samples to be analyzed in a lab.

To take a blood sample, an ER tech first locates a vein to draw blood from. They usually choose a site on the inside of the elbow or the back of the hand. Next, the tech cleans the site. This kills any germs on the skin and protects the patient from infections. The tech then ties a band around the patient's upper arm, causing the vein below the band to swell with blood. Then the tech inserts a hollow needle into the vein. Blood flows through the needle and collects in a tube. Then the tube is delivered to the lab.

HEALING & MOBILITY AIDS

Many ER patients have broken bones, sprains, or other injuries relating to their muscles or skeletons. ER techs help fit these patients with casts or splints. These devices keep the injured part of the body stable and supported so it can heal properly. ER techs also fit patients with crutches, wheelchairs, and other mobility aids that allow patients to move while they heal.

FEEDING TUBES & CATHETERS

An ER tech may assist with inserting and removing a feeding tube. This is a thin tube that runs from a patient's nose to their stomach. This tube is used to deliver food or medicine to a patient who cannot chew or swallow. It can also be used to draw out stomach contents.

ER techs also assist with inserting and removing urinary catheters. A urinary catheter is a thin tube inserted through the urethra and into the bladder. It is used to drain urine from the bladder. This helps patients who can't pee on their own or have lost control of their bladder.

HOUSEKEEPING

When they aren't with patients, ER techs work hard to keep the ER functioning. They clean rooms and change bedding between patients. They disinfect medical instruments and restock supplies and medicines. Performing these housekeeping duties keeps the ER organized, sanitized, and ready for any emergency.

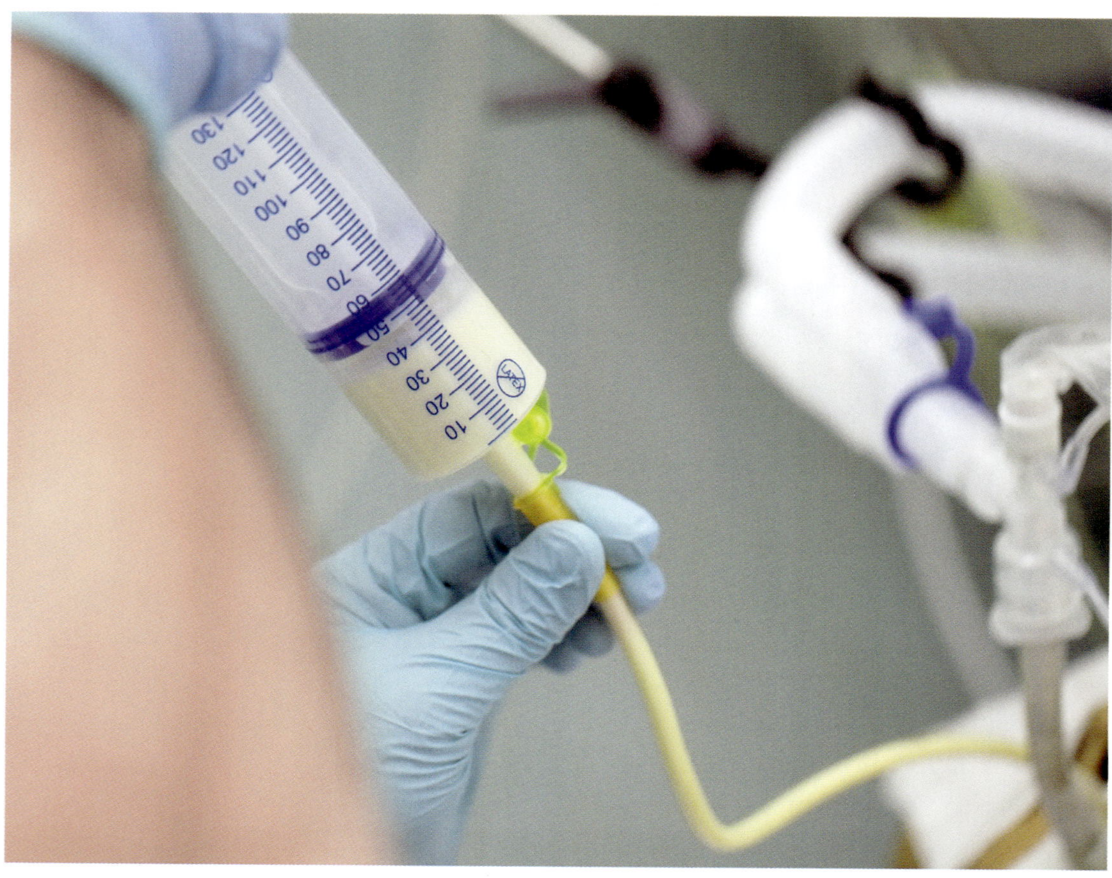

ER techs also work to make sure patients are comfortable and reassure them if needed.

Community paramedics can provide many different services. These include disease management, preventative and wellness care, mental health care, oral health care, health education, injury care, and more.

Community paramedics usually carry a bag with an assortment of basic medical supplies they may need to help a sick patient.

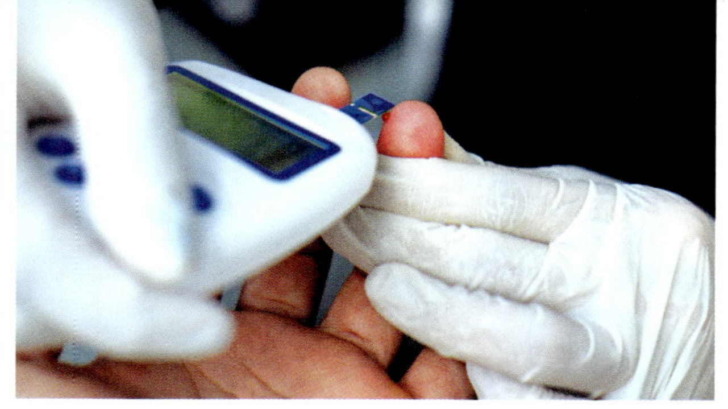

COMMUNITY PARAMEDIC

Community paramedics are trained to provide primary care in addition to emergency care. Primary care is medical care that helps promote wellness, prevent illness, and manage chronic conditions. By providing this type of care outside of traditional clinic settings, community paramedics improve the health of vulnerable and underserved populations. This leads to fewer people in need of ambulance and ER services.

VULNERABLE & UNDERSERVED

Community paramedics provide health services for a variety of patients. Some are individuals who need follow-up care after being discharged from a hospital. Others are those at risk of needing hospital services if they don't receive regular care. Community paramedics also serve individuals who aren't able to travel to a primary care clinic. This can be due to lack of transportation or other resources. These patients need health care workers who can come to them. That's why, in addition to working at clinics and hospitals, community paramedics also provide services in patients' homes, residential care facilities, and shelters.

PRIMARY CARE

Community paramedics provide a variety of primary care services to the populations they serve. One of these services is conducting health assessments. A health assessment is a set of questions a health care provider asks a patient about their lifestyle and behaviors. The questions cover topics such as diet, physical activity, and safety issues. These assessments help community paramedics understand a patient's overall health. It also helps them develop a plan for the patient's ongoing care.

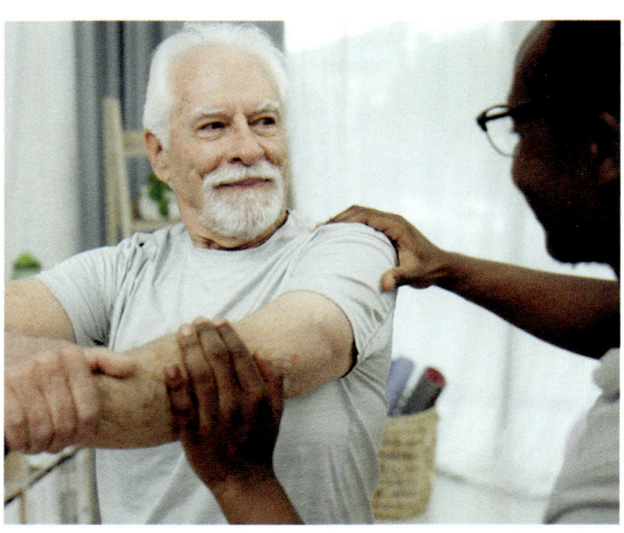

Community paramedics also help patients manage chronic diseases. For example, a community paramedic might help a patient with diabetes monitor their blood sugar. They may also help create a plan to keep it under control through medication, diet, and lifestyle choices. Patients can also rely on community paramedics to collect samples, such as blood and urine samples, and transport them to labs for analysis. Beyond managing illness and disease, community paramedics help promote wellness with services like health education.

COMMUNITY COLLABORATION

Community paramedics work with other services to give their patients the care they need. For example, a community paramedic may work with a local homelessness assistance program to help a patient experiencing homelessness. Or they might provide a patient with transportation to another health service provider. This could be a mental health clinic or addiction recovery center. It takes a team effort to keep a community healthy!

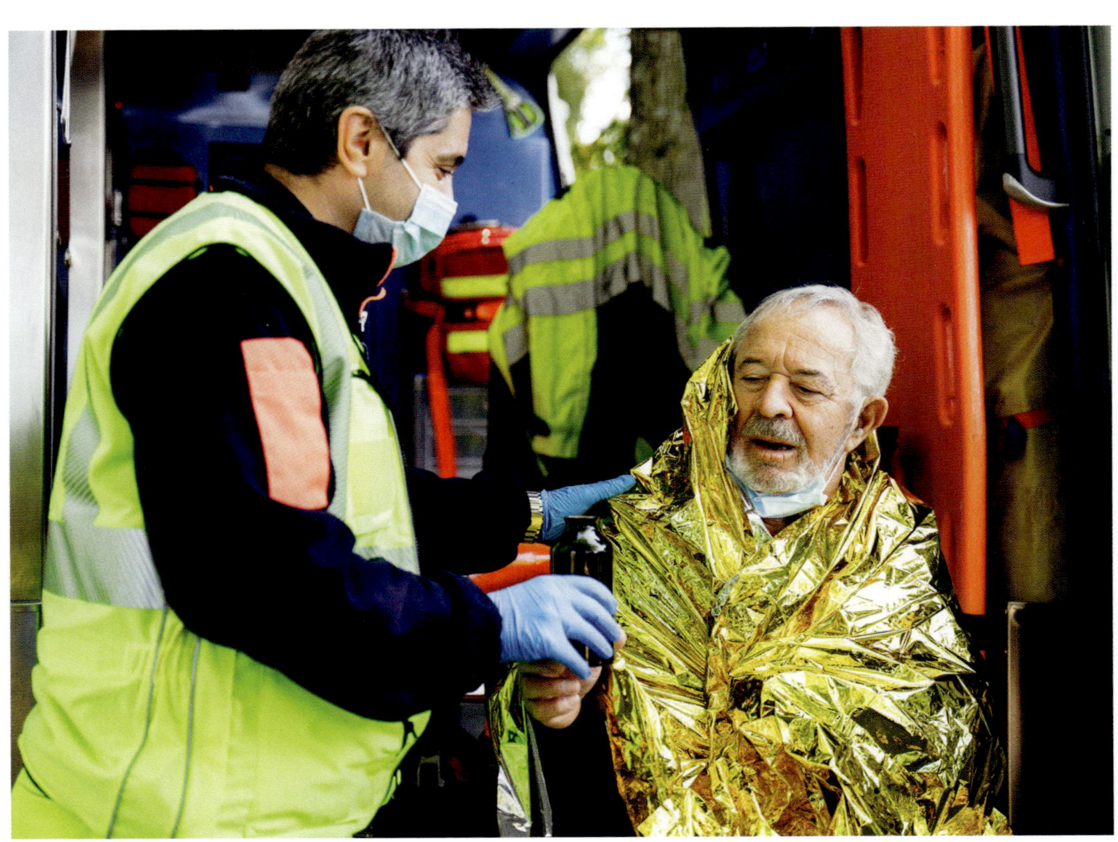

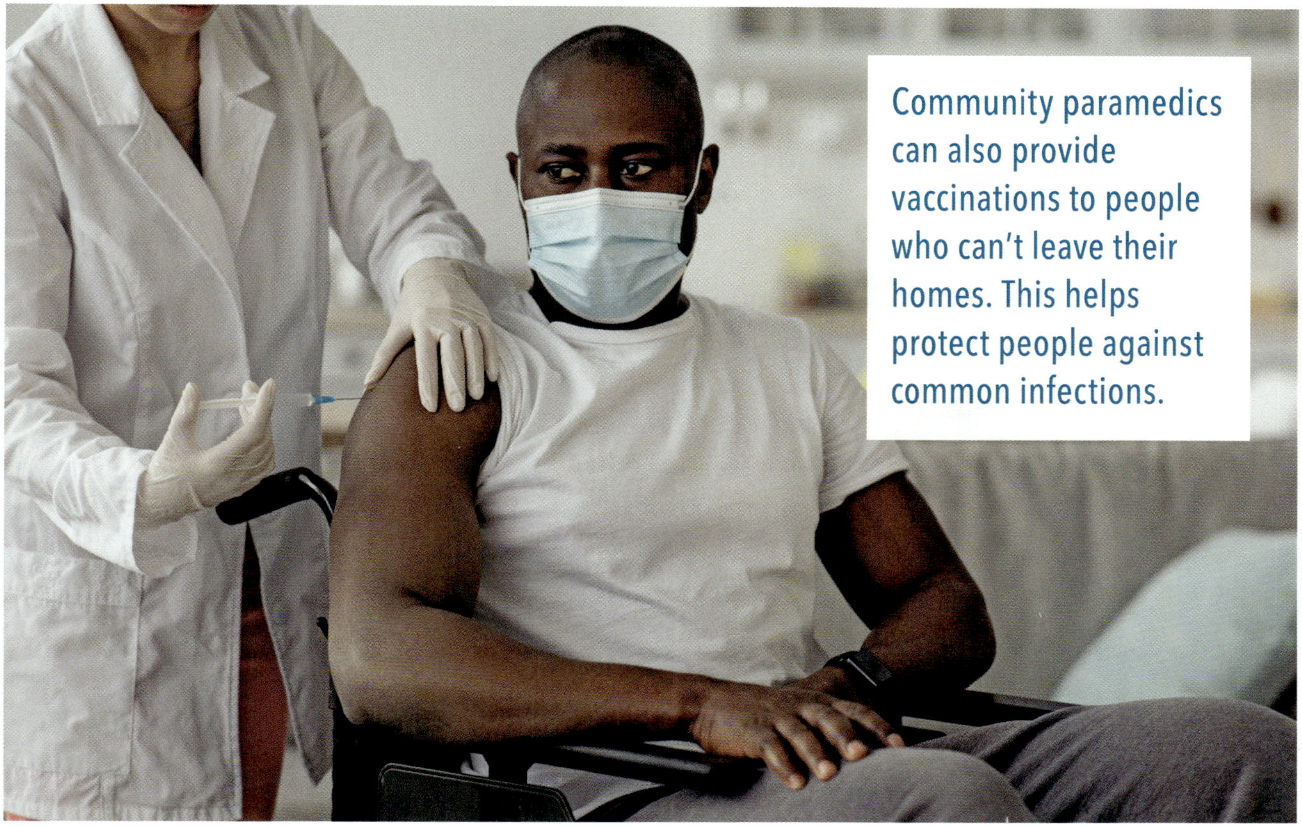

Community paramedics can also provide vaccinations to people who can't leave their homes. This helps protect people against common infections.

During the COVID-19 pandemic, community paramedics provided medical assistance at vaccination sites.

CREATE YOUR VISION

It's time to get creative! What interests you about emergency medical services? Create a vision board that inspires you. Let it motivate you to turn your talents into your trade!

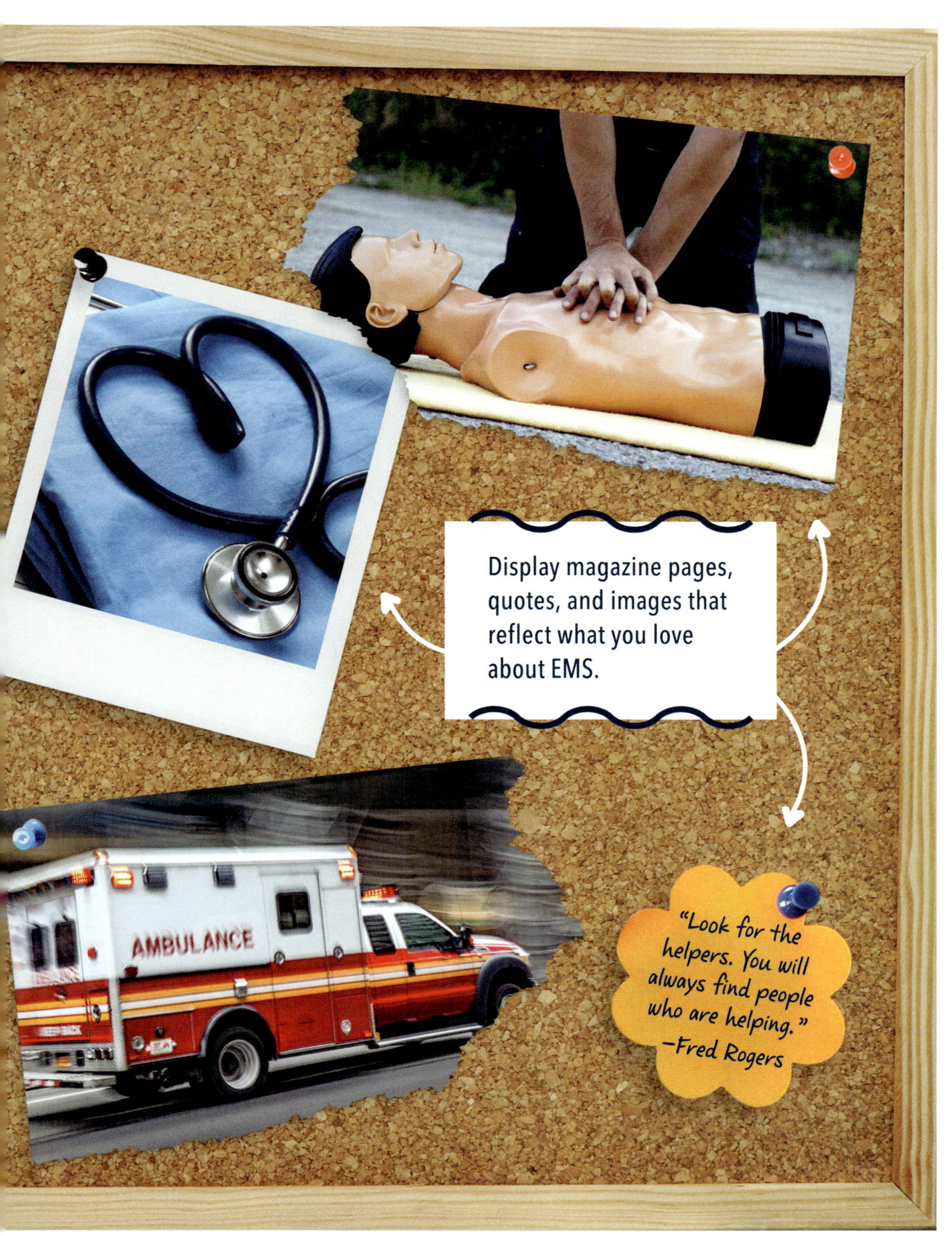
Display magazine pages, quotes, and images that reflect what you love about EMS.
"Look for the helpers. You will always find people who are helping."
—Fred Rogers
AMBULANCE

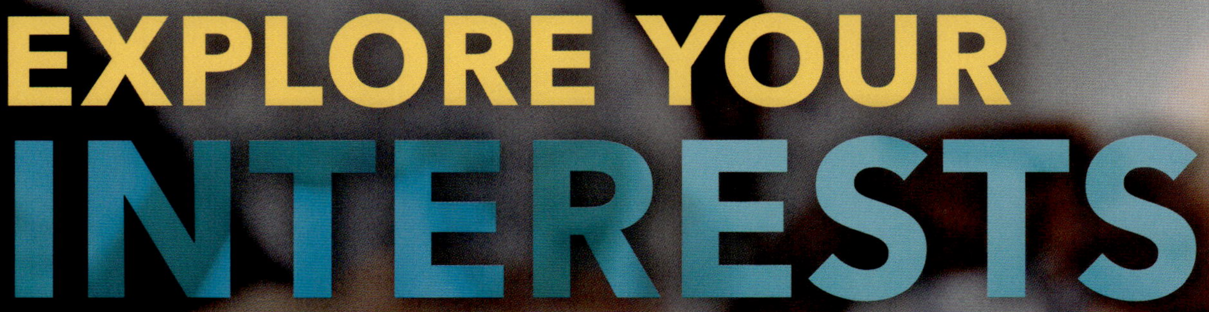

EXPLORE YOUR INTERESTS

You've got the passion, vision, and motivation. Now it's time to learn! Find high school electives and community courses that could give you relevant knowledge to reach your goals.

Take a psychology or sociology class to better understand people and their behaviors. This skill is important when interacting with patients.

Take a CPR course at your school or in your community to learn the lifesaving procedure.

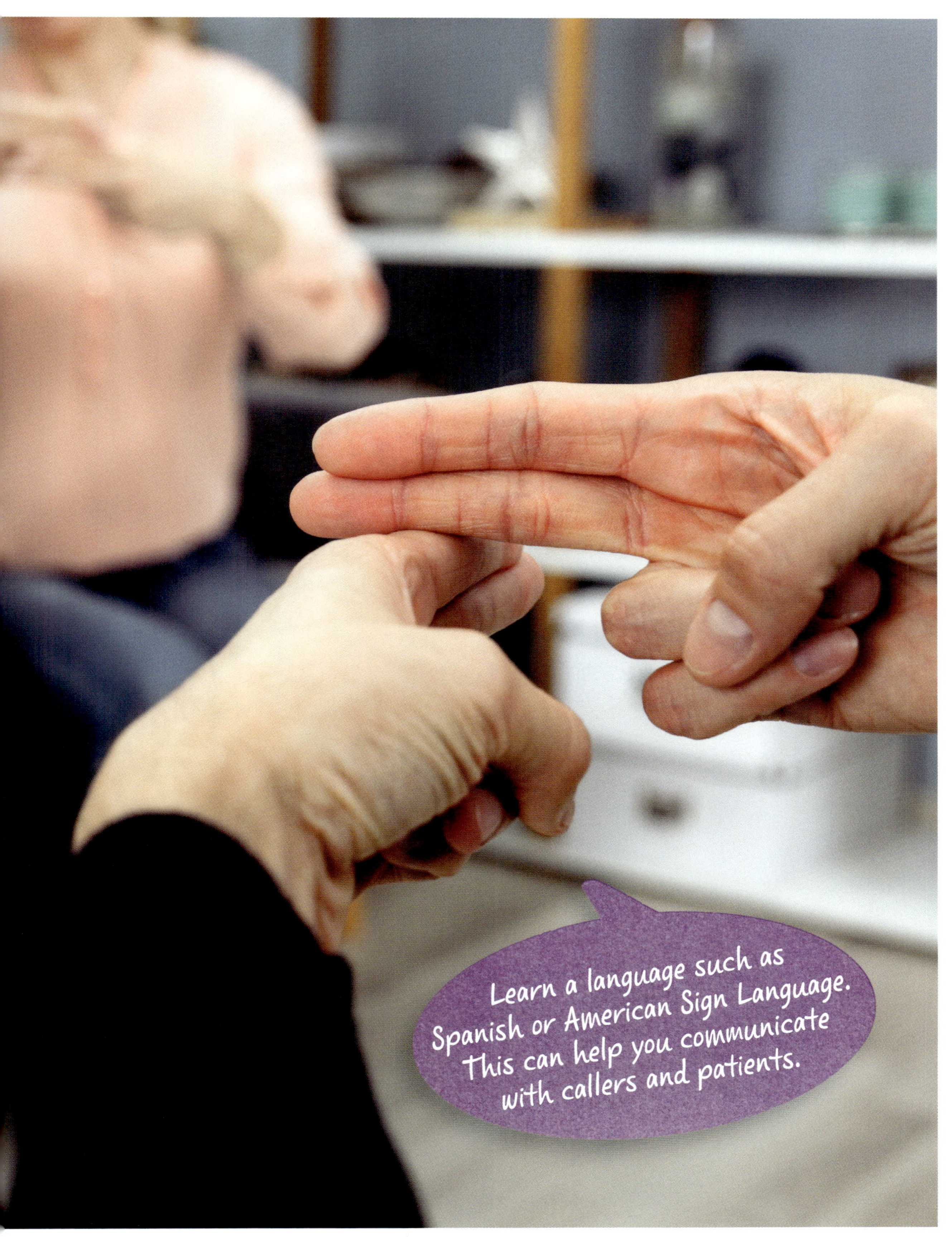
Learn a language such as
Spanish or American Sign Language.
This can help you communicate
with callers and patients.

ENHANCE YOUR ABILITIES

Think about what you can work on in your free time. Even if you aren't ready to start formal training, you can still develop your technical and transferable skills. Transferable skills include communication, leadership, and more!

If you want to be a dispatcher, practice interpreting maps and giving clear directions to others.

Get familiar with first aid kits and how to properly use the items in them.

Practice prioritizing tasks by creating to-do lists. Put urgent items first and consider if any tasks can be delayed or delegated.

BUILD YOUR RÉSUMÉ

Find a part-time job or volunteer opportunity that gives you experience relevant to your future role. Include these positions and your responsibilities within them on your résumé.

Work at a call center or as a receptionist who takes customer calls or books appointments.

Work with people outside your age group, such as young children or senior citizens. This often requires clearer, more thoughtful communication.

Become a lifeguard, hospital volunteer, or junior firefighter.

CREATE YOUR OWN FIRST AID KITS

Prepare for any emergencies at home or on the go by making your own first aid kits!

SUPPLIES

plastic container with lid
ruler
scissors
paper
card stock
markers
clear tape
washi tape or patterned paper (optional)
clear packing tape
first aid items
small empty metal or plastic box
mini first aid kit items

STEPS

1 Measure the container's lid. Cut a piece of paper that is about 1 inch (2.5 cm) shorter on all sides.

2 To create the label, cut a piece of card stock that can fit within the paper from step 1. Write "First Aid" on the card stock. Leave space for a cross. Tape the card stock to the paper. Make a cross with two identical pieces of washi tape or patterned paper. You can also draw a cross. A red cross is a common symbol for first aid.

3 Attach the label to the container's lid with clear packing tape. Completely cover the label with tape to make it water resistant.

4 Gather and add the supplies below to the kit.
- adhesive bandages
- elastic bandages
- antibiotic ointment
- hand sanitizer
- other first aid items
- tweezers
- sunscreen
- flashlight
- cold pack

5 Basic medications, such as pain relief and allergy relief, make great additions to any first aid kit. Check the expiration dates periodically and replace them if they are expired. Also consider your family's needs. For example, if someone has an EpiPen or prescription medication, include it in the kit.

6 Place the kit in an easy-to-locate spot in your house or the family car for when you need it! Use an empty bandage box to make a mini version of the first aid kit for your backpack or purse.

BECOMING AN EMS SPECIALIST

TRAINING

Are you ready for your formal training to be an EMS specialist? Most EMS employers require job applicants to have at least a high school diploma. Further training and certification requirements vary based on the occupation and state.

Most emergency dispatchers are trained by their employers. The requirements and length of training vary by state. But most programs include educational courses and on-the-job training. Dispatchers also learn how to use CAD systems. Additionally, some states require dispatchers to pass a typing test and a certification exam. And some dispatchers need special certifications so they can provide medical assistance to callers. For

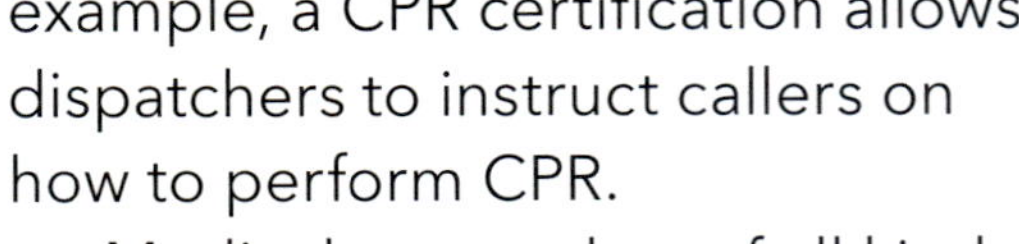

example, a CPR certification allows dispatchers to instruct callers on how to perform CPR.

Medical responders of all kinds must complete a training program and become EMT certified. The amount of training required depends on the role. Most colleges, universities, technical institutes, and medical training facilities offer EMT certification programs.

EMTs and ER technicians need about 120 hours of training. Paramedics usually need as much as 1,800 hours or more. Most employers also require paramedics to work as an EMT before starting to train as a paramedic. And many paramedics get an associate's or bachelor's degree in paramedicine.

Community paramedics usually need to have previous paramedic experience. They also need additional training in nonemergency health care. Many colleges, universities, and medical training facilities offer community paramedicine programs or certificates. Some community paramedics also get additional certifications to meet the specific needs of the community they help.

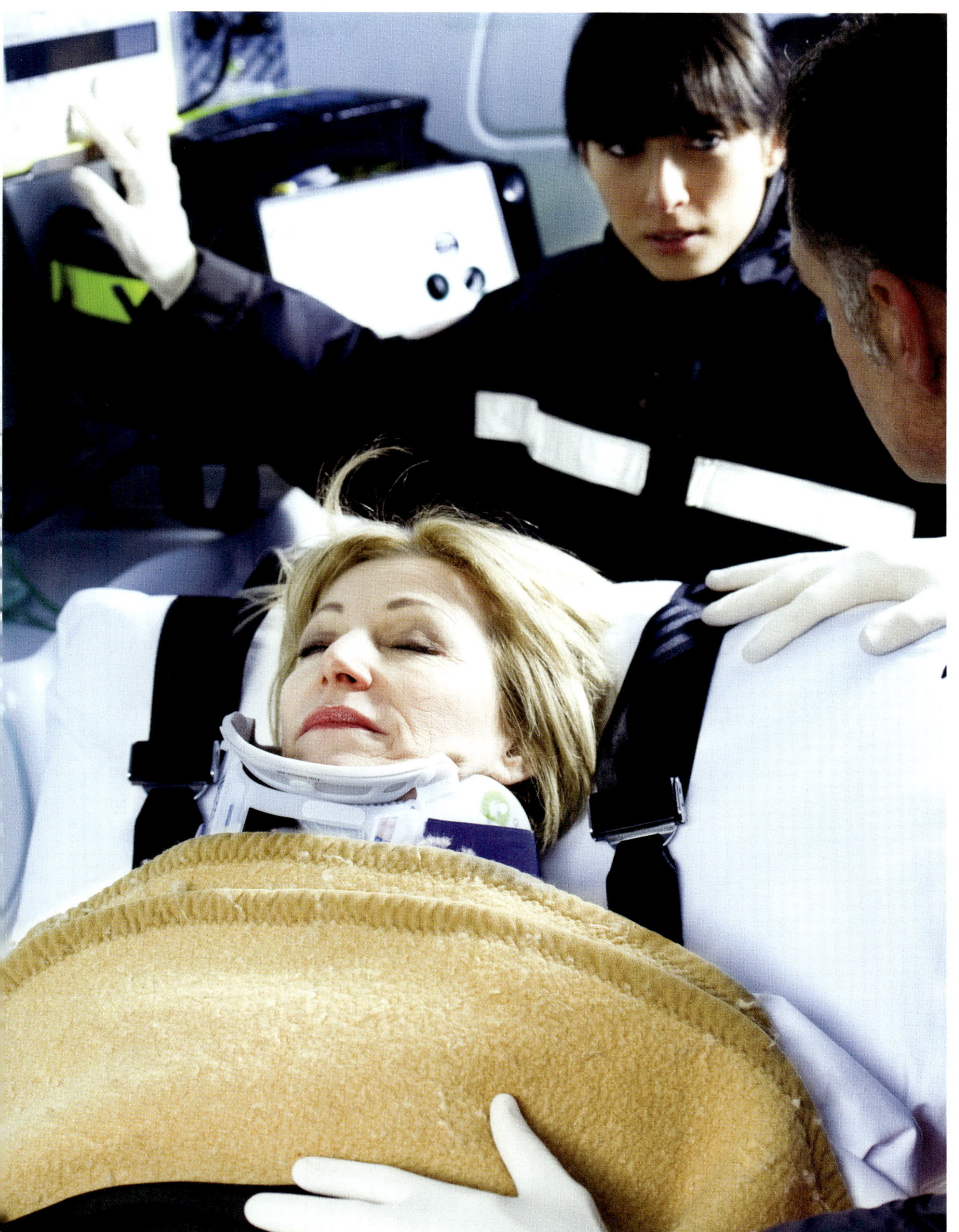

PRE-EMPLOYMENT SCREENING

EMS specialists often work in life-and-death situations. So most EMS employers screen prospective employees. This ensures they are mentally and physically fit for the job. Pre-employment screenings can include background checks and lie detector tests. These give employers information about a person's criminal history, driving records, employment history, and more. Other screenings include hearing, vision, and drug tests.

CAREER PROGRESSION

Education and training don't stop once you land your first job. Medical responders of all kinds must periodically complete courses to stay updated on their knowledge and skills. They must also take exams to renew their certification on a regular basis. In some states, emergency dispatchers must also complete additional training throughout their careers.

EMTs and paramedics usually need to renew their certification every two years.

MEET SOME PROS: THE NATION'S FIRST PARAMEDICS

Up until the late 1960s, ambulances primarily transported patients to hospitals. But many didn't provide patient care. The lack of proper prehospital care led to many preventable deaths. This began to change in 1967 thanks to the Freedom House Ambulance Service.

Freedom House was established to provide an ambulance service for the Hill District. The Hill District was an underserved Black community in Pittsburgh, Pennsylvania. The service also addressed unemployment in the Hill District. It did this by recruiting and training community members to work as paramedics. The recruits underwent intensive training in a wide range of emergency medical procedures. This included anything from treating heart attacks to delivering babies.

Freedom House was soon recognized across the country and beyond as the standard for prehospital care. Despite the program's success, the city of Pittsburgh eventually decided to defund it. They replaced it with a citywide ambulance service made up of mostly white paramedics. Freedom House was largely forgotten to history until journalist and former paramedic Kevin Hazzard brought its story to light. He wrote about Freedom House in his 2022 book *American Sirens: The Incredible Story of the Black Men Who Became America's First Paramedics*.

Freedom House Ambulance Service employees in the 1970s

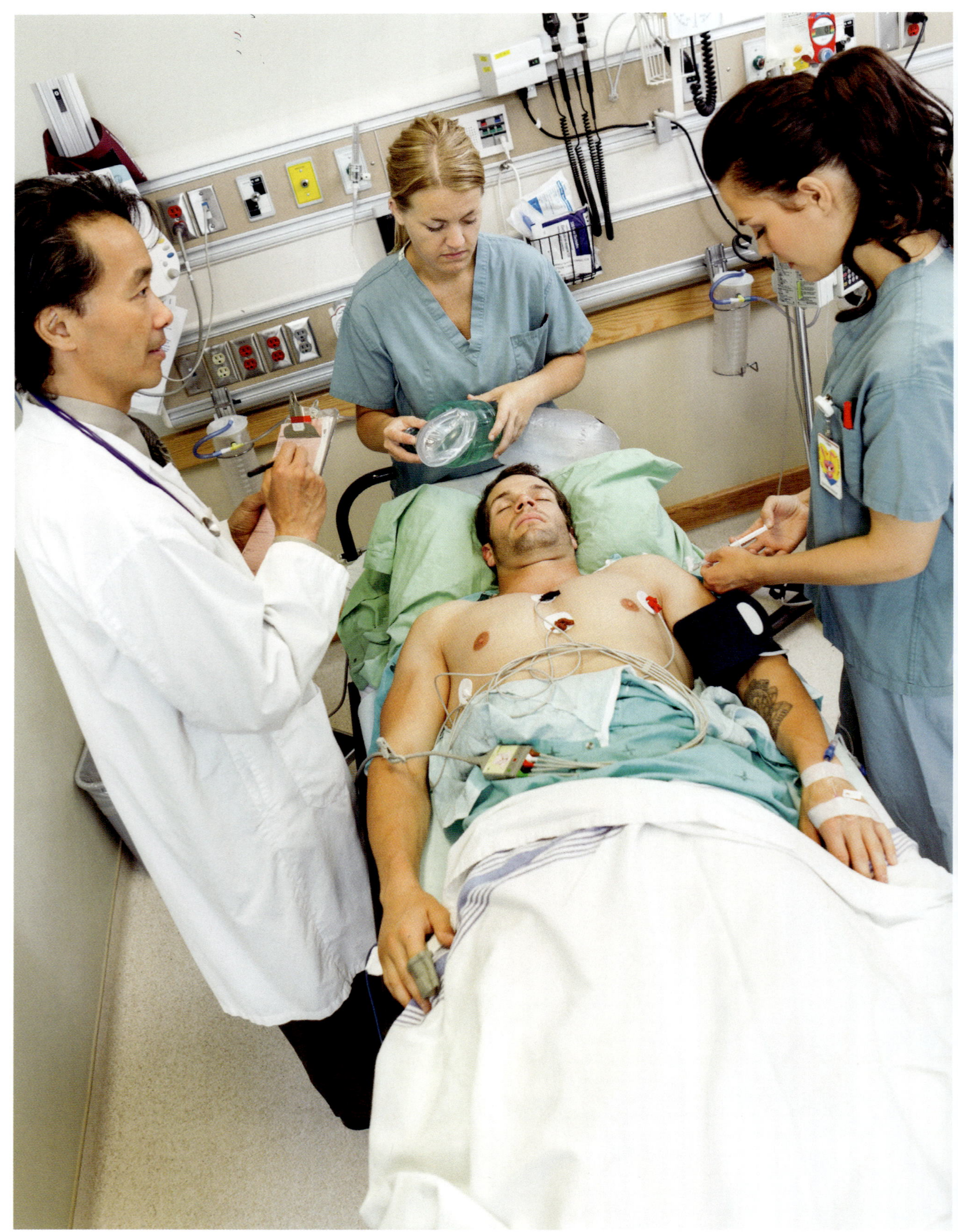

TRADES AT WORK

EARNING POTENTIAL

The US Bureau of Labor Statistics provides estimated wage ranges for most workers in a given job category. The average salaries below are from May 2023. While these estimates provide a sense of what you could expect to earn, actual salaries can vary greatly depending on where you work, your amount of experience, and any specialized skills you have.

GROW YOUR POTENTIAL

Whatever salary you start at, there are various ways to grow your earning potential throughout your career. Here are a few ways to boost your income while continuing to do what you love.

Consider a new EMS role. An emergency dispatcher may decide to complete EMT training so they can help people face-to-face. An EMT may transition to working in a hospital as an ER technician. And a paramedic could expand their role by training to become a community paramedic.

Become a contract medic. Contract medics are paramedics and EMTs who are hired to work short-term or seasonal jobs.

JOB CATEGORY	ANNUAL SALARY
Public Safety Telecommunicators	$40,000-$61,000
Emergency Medical Technicians	$35,000-$47,000
Paramedics	$46,000-$64,000
Emergency Room Technicians	$36,000-$51,000*
Community Paramedics	$44,000-$61,000*

** The Bureau of Labor Statistics does not provide salary information for emergency room technicians or community paramedics. The estimated wage ranges for these jobs are provided by a nongovernment source.*

Cruise ships, music festivals, and amusement parks are examples of settings that host many people and therefore require medics who are on-site in case of an emergency. Medics are also hired to work on offshore oil rigs, at remote manufacturing plants, and in other industrial environments where injuries can be serious and regular emergency services are not nearby.

Go back to school. An ER technician may discover they want to go to medical school to become a surgeon. An EMT may decide to go to nursing school. A community paramedic could develop an interest in mental health and go back to school to become a psychologist. Going back to school is costly and time-consuming. But it's easier to make the commitment when you're passionate about what you're learning and you have a clear goal in mind.

FINANCIAL SMARTS

However you're making money, it's important to manage your finances wisely. If you have an employer, you will receive a regular paycheck from them. This income will be your wages minus taxes. If your employer offers health insurance, retirement savings, or any other benefits, those will also be deducted from your take-home pay. Financial experts recommend you put about 20 percent of each paycheck into savings and try to keep an emergency fund with three to six months' worth of living expenses.

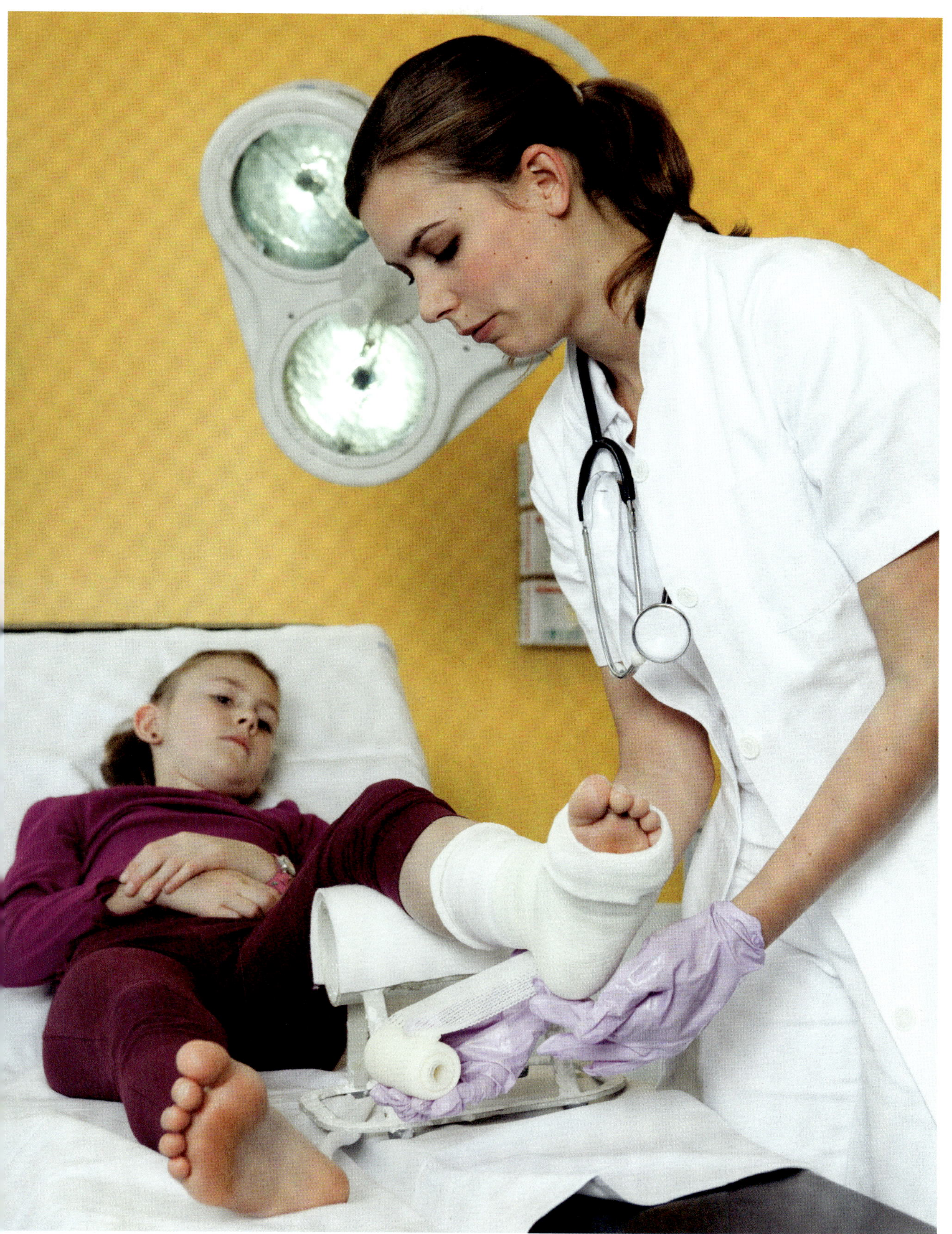

-?-
8:39

DO WHAT YOU LOVE!

Being an EMS specialist requires compassion, flexibility, teamwork, and more. Finding success in this work can take years of training and a commitment to keep learning and growing your skills. Many EMS specialists find the time and effort are worth the rewards of helping those who are in trouble.

Maybe your goal is to care for patients as a paramedic or EMT. Maybe you have your sights set on working in an ER. Or perhaps you want to coordinate first responders as an emergency dispatcher. As long as you do what you love, you'll love what you do!

GLOSSARY

analgesic–a drug that helps relieve pain.

analyze–to examine something to find out what it is or what makes it work. Analysis is the process or result of analyzing something.

assess–to determine the importance, value, or condition of something. An assessment is the process or result of assessing something.

automation–the change from manual control to computer control.

chronic–occurring frequently or for a very long time.

diabetes–a disease in which the body cannot properly process normal amounts of sugar and starch.

diagnose–to identify something, such as a disease, by signs, symptoms, or tests.

dispatch–to send someone or something to a particular place for a particular purpose. A person who does this is a dispatcher.

efficiency–the ability to produce a desired result, especially without wasting time or energy.

elective–a class that counts toward graduation but is not required.

entity–a business or government organization.

epinephrine–a hormone that helps counter the effects of an allergic reaction.

glucose–a naturally occurring form of sugar found in plants, fruits, and blood.

inadequate–not good enough.

integrate–to combine with or add to something else.

intravenous–inside of or entering a vein.

monitor–to watch, keep track of, or oversee.

musculoskeletal–relating to both the muscles and skeleton.

periodic–repeating at regular intervals of time.

personnel–the people employed by a certain organization.

potential–capable of being or becoming, or something that could be.

prioritize–put the most important item or task first.

saline—made of or containing salt.

specialize—to develop expertise in a certain area, called a specialty. A person who does this is a specialist.

stamina—the power to endure fatigue, disease, or hardship.

technical—related to special knowledge of how a particular kind of work is done. A technician or tech is someone who is skilled at a task requiring special knowledge. A technique is a way of doing a task using special knowledge or skills.

urethra—a passage where urine leaves the body from the bladder.

vertebrae—tiny bones that make up the backbone.

World War I—from 1914 to 1918, fought in Europe. Great Britain, France, Russia, the United States, and their allies were on one side. Germany, Austria-Hungary, and their allies were on the other side.

ONLINE RESOURCES

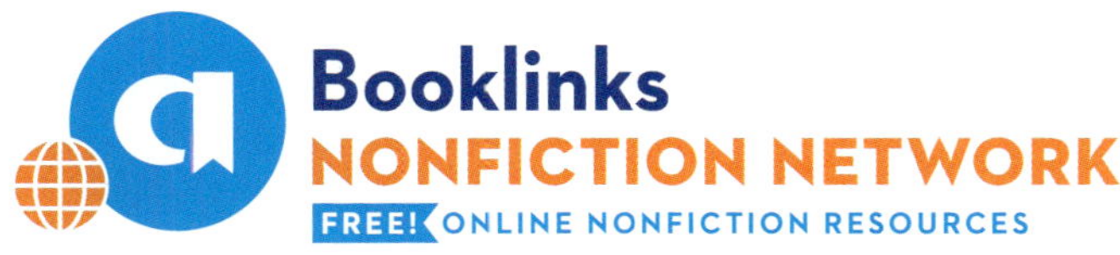

To learn more about trades in EMS, please visit **abdobooklinks.com** or scan this QR code. These links are routinely monitored and updated to provide the most current information available.

INDEX